AMERICAN CULTURE AND RELIGION

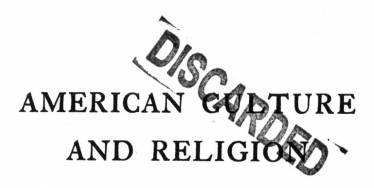

AMERICAN CULTURE AND RELIGION

Six Essays

BY WILLIAM WARREN SWEET

NEW YORK
COOPER SQUARE PUBLISHERS, INC.
1972

Originally Published and Copyright, 1951 by
Southern Methodist University Press
Reprinted by Permission of Southern Methodist University Press
Published 1972 by Cooper Square Publishers, Inc.
59 Fourth Avenue, New York, N. Y. 10003
International Standard Book No. 0-8154-0421-2
Library of Congress Catalog Card No. 72-78372

Printed in the United States of America

Dedicated

to

JOHN NELSON RUSSELL SCORE

President

Southwestern University

1942-1949

and to

JOSEPH J. *and* LOIS PERKINS

generous benefactors

of both

Southwestern and

Southern Methodist Universities

PREFACE

THESE essays on the general theme of American Culture and Religion were presented as the Southwestern University Lectures for 1947. The first, "Cultural Pluralism in the American Tradition," was also read before the Institute for Religion and Social Studies in Chicago in January, 1944, and was published in *Christendom* in 1946. The second, "Protestantism and Democracy," was originally given as an address at the seventy-fifth anniversary of Wesley College in Winnipeg, Canada, in 1945. The third, "Natural Religion and Religious Liberty," was the Dudlean Lecture at Harvard University in 1944 and appeared in the *Harvard Divinity School Bulletin* the following year.

The fourth essay, "Methodist Unification," originally appeared in *Religion in the Making*. The fifth, "The Church, the Sect, and the Cult in America," was published in the Winter, 1951, issue of *Southwest Review*. The sixth, "Ecumenicity Begins at Home," was the opening address at Garrett Biblical Institute in the autumn of 1947.

W. W. S.

CONTENTS

1

CULTURAL PLURALISM IN THE AMERICAN
TRADITION

A MERICA abounds in contradictions. We are im-
mensely proud of the fact that our country has
been a haven of the persecuted and oppressed of the
world throughout all our history, and yet we have
developed a pattern of racial prejudice more compli-
cated than that which is to be found in any other nation
on earth. The very fact that we have thrown open our
doors to all is the basic explanation for these contradictory attitudes and for the prevailing race antago-
nisms with which we are all only too familiar.[1] I think
we can reasonably assume that any other people exposed
to the same set of historic influences would have come
out about where we are today in race attitudes. For race
antagonism is no monopoly of any one so-called race.
Bring together in any one land all the various peoples
of the world, differing in color, speech, religion, and
cultural, political, and economic background, as well as
in standards of living, and you set the stage for inevi-

[1] I use the term "race" as commonly understood by the average person, and not in the scientific sense. The scientist has concluded that
there are no such things as distinct races. See M. F. A. Montagu, *Man's
Most Dangerous Myth: The Fallacy of Race* (New York: Columbia
University Press, 1942).

[1]

table conflict. It would be strange, indeed, if this were not true.

Cultural pluralism is a social philosophy which attributes value and validity to other cultures than one's own. In the case of the United States it is the point of view which would implement this social philosophy by encouraging the preservation of the cultural values among the immigrants who have come to our shores. Our history is replete with instances of the influence of other cultures mingling in the United States, but this has come about without any conscious plan. Until recent years we meant by "Americanization" elimination as far as possible of other cultural influences and values than our own. There is need for the development of an appreciation of all that the many nationals have contributed to the advancement of America. To develop this appreciation adequately we must have an educational program which will furnish the chance for each to achieve all that he is capable of achieving regardless of race or nationality, rather than one designed to eliminate other cultural values.[2]

II

Racial and cultural diversity has been characteristic of America from the beginning. It is true that the first colonies established in America—Virginia, the New England group, and Maryland—were practically 100

[2]Francis J. Brown and Joseph S. Roucek (eds.), *Our Racial and National Minorities, Their History, Contributions and Present Problems* (New York, 1937), pp. 752-53.

per cent English, at least until toward the close of the seventeenth century. But at the beginning of the eighteenth century foreign immigration made up a good share of the people who were turning their faces toward the new promised land. America and the colonies established after that time drew their population from many countries. The population of all the colonies in 1690 has been estimated at a quarter of a million; from that time forward until the end of the colonial period the population doubled every twenty-five years, until at the opening of the War for Independence in 1775 the population of the thirteen colonies included more than ten times that number, or two and a half million souls. And a large proportion of this vast increase was due to the coming of the "foreigner." At least one-third of the population in 1775 was foreign born.

In the establishment of the earlier colonies religion had been a dominant motive. The great eighteenth-century immigration was largely impelled by economic considerations. The following penetrating observations as to the kind of people making up the bulk of this immigration are from the *Letters from an American Farmer*[3] written by Jean de Crèvecoeur, a French-American who had married an American wife and, in the 1760's, had settled in Orange County, New York,

---

[3]Michel Guillaume Jean de Crèvecoeur, *Letters from an American Farmer* (London, 1782), pp. 52-55, 75-76. These letters are published under the name "J. Hector St. John," a name which the author occasionally used "simply because he likes it." See *Dictionary of American Biography*, Vol. IV, article by Stanley T. Williams.

then a new frontier. These observations are based on his own experiences as an explorer and a frontier farmer:

The rich stay in Europe, it is only the middling and the poor that emigrate. In this great American asylum, the poor of Europe have by some means met together, and in consequence of various causes; to what purpose should they ask one another what countrymen they are? Alas, two thirds of them had no country. Can a wretch who wanders about, who works and starves . . . can that man call England or any other kingdom his country? A country that had no bread for him, whose fields procured him no harvest, who met with nothing but the frowns of the rich, the severity of the laws, with jails and punishments; who owned not a single foot of the extensive surface of this planet? No! Urged by a variety of motives, here they came.

Once they had planted their feet on American soil:

Every thing has tended to regenerate them; new laws, a new mode of living, a new social system; here they are become men: in Europe they were as so many useless plants, wanting vegitative mould, and refreshing showers; they withered, and were mowed down by want, hunger, and war; but now by the power of transplantation, like all other plants they have taken root and flourished! Formerly they were not numbered in any civil lists of their country, except in those of the poor; here they rank as citizens. By what invisible power has this surprising metamorphosis been performed? By that of the laws and that of their industry . . . his country is now that which gives him land, bread, protection, and consequence: *Ubi panis ibi patria* [Where there is bread, there is my country], is the motto of all emigrants. . . . Here the rewards of his industry follow with equal steps the progress of his labour.

There can be no doubt that the economic motive was the principal one which brought a great majority of eighteenth-century immigrants to America. But it was not the only one. Mingled with it were political and religious persecution and unrest, and here and there among the immigrants were those who, while thinking

[4]

of bettering their economic status, had in their minds and hearts a consuming desire to build a better and higher life for themselves and their children.

III

The principal non-English-speaking people who came to America during the colonial period were the Dutch, the Swedes, the French Huguenots, and the Germans.

The Dutch came to America as traders, and the Dutch West India Company,[4] the agency which established New Netherland, was no benevolent organization. The company was organized to trade with the Indians, not to convert them, and the transplanting of the Dutch Reformed church to America was a mere incident and a decidedly secondary by-product. Yet when the English finally took over New Netherland in 1664 thirteen Dutch Reformed churches had been established, and by the end of the colonial period the number of Dutch congregations had grown to at least a hundred, in all of which the service and the sermons were still largely in Dutch.

The tenacity with which the Dutch clung to their worship in the Dutch language and the dependence of their churches upon the Classis of Amsterdam explain

[4]For a recent appraisal of Dutch colonial contributions see T. J. Wertenbaker, *The Founding of American Civilization: The Middle Colonies* (New York, 1938), especially chaps. ii and iii. For an interesting statement as to the persistence of Dutch influence in New York City after independence see J. B. McMaster, *A History of the People of the United States*, I, 55-56 (New York, 1900). See also Carl Wittke, *We Who Built America* (New York, 1939), pp. 14-22.

for the most part the fact that the Dutch were not quickly absorbed, and that they remained for so long a time a distinct cultural element in New York City and in the Hudson Valley. Though continuing as an element apart, the Dutch were influential in the government of the colony of New York even after it was taken over by the English, and had in general equal social and political standing with the English. Even in the eighteenth century to be known as of Dutch extraction was no handicap socially, economically, or politically; nor has it been since, as the long list of distinguished Dutch names in our history will testify. Among them are three presidents of the United States—Van Buren and the two Roosevelts—and sixty members of Congress.[5]

The Dutch influence in architecture, customs, and geography still persists. The word *Kill*, meaning creek, is commonly used in New York, New Jersey, and Delaware. Dutch colonial domestic architecture is now popular in all sections of the country and has added much to the beauty of new residential developments. Ministers of all denominations are still called *Domines* on Long Island and up the Hudson. Dutch thrift, neat-

---

[5]The Livingston family furnishes an illustration of the result of the mingling of the Dutch strain in our history. Robert Livingston, the founder of the family in America, and the first Lord of Livingston Manor on the Hudson, was the son of a Scotch Presbyterian minister who fled to Holland, like many another religious refugee. Here Robert learned the Dutch language, and when he came to Albany in 1674 he soon gained public office. Five years later he married the widow of Domine Nicholas Van Rensselaer, the sister of Peter Schuyler. See the biographies of eight descendants in the *Dictionary of American Biography*, Vol. XI.

ness, and cleanliness, for which colonial Dutch house-
wives were famous, are no mean heritage. A Hessian
who served in the American Revolution has left this
account of the Dutch farmers in the southern counties
of New York:

> The inhabited parts . . . are built up with the most beautiful houses,
> situated on the most agreeable sites. Their furniture would satisfy the
> finest tastes, and is of a quality that we cannot boast of at home. At the
> same time, everything is so clean and shining that I can hardly describe
> it.[6]

In 1697 there were about twelve hundred people on
the Delaware who spoke Swedish, besides a considerable
sprinkling of Finns. Several Swedish Lutheran congregations were formed, which retained connections with
Sweden until the middle of the eighteenth century, the
ministers being sent from Sweden. The Swedes constituted a small but sturdy element in the population; but
their numbers were too few to resist rapid amalgamation, and by the end of the colonial era there was little
to indicate their cultural contribution. At the close of
the Revolution one of the few Swedish ministers still
remaining lamented that "these descendants of the
Swedes . . . have no more affection for anything from
Sweden than if it were from Turkey."[7]

The French Huguenots, constituting about fifteen

[6]Helen E. Smith, *Colonial Days and Ways* (New York, 1900),
pp. 117-19. Quoted in Wittke, *op. cit.*, p. 16. See also H. T. Collen-
brander, "The Dutch Element in American History" in *American
History Association Report* (1909), pp. 193-201, and Ruth Putnam,
"The Dutch Element in the United States," *ibid.*, pp. 218 ff.

[7]Wittke, *op. cit.*, pp. 35-38; also William Warren Sweet, *Religion
in Colonial America*, pp. 203-5.

thousand all told, probably furnished a larger number of people of capacity and culture in proportion to their numbers than any other non-English-speaking group in the colonial period. This fact largely accounts for their rapid assimilation, for they were soon occupying places of influence, and their rapid economic rehabilitation made easy their intermarriage with English-speaking people of their own economic and social status. There were some four thousand Huguenots in New England in 1700, and from them came Paul Revere and the Faneuil brothers, one of whom, Peter, was, next to John Hancock, the most important merchant in Revolutionary New England. It was he who built and presented to the city of Boston Faneuil Hall, the "cradle of liberty." John Greenleaf Whittier's mother was a descendant of Huguenots. James Bowdoin, governor of Massachusetts, who gave his name to the oldest college in Maine, was a descendant of Pierre Baudouin, a Huguenot refugee who came to Maine in the year 1687, and whose descendants became wealthy and influential merchants.[8]

New Rochelle, New York, founded under the leadership of the French Huguenot minister, David Bourepos, was a center of Huguenot influence in New York. The town achieved local fame for its schools, where English-speaking families sent their boys to learn the

[8] See articles in the *Dictionary of American Biography* on James Bowdoin, Peter Faneuil, John Greenleaf Whittier. Whittier's mother's family had changed its name from Feuillevert to Greenleaf. For the frequency of such changes of names see Wittke, *op. cit.*, pp. 25-26.

French language and French manners. Among those who were scholars there were Washington Irving, John Jay, and Gouverneur Morris. Nor were the young gentlemen the only ones to profit from this center of French culture, for there were also schools for young ladies where music, painting, embroidery, and etiquette were taught after the French manner. The largest Huguenot colony in colonial America, however, was that in South Carolina, where six French colonial churches were established. The story of their influence has been told in detail by Professor A. H. Hirsch in his *The Huguenots of Colonial South Carolina.*[9] It is astonishing with what rapidity they became leaders in the economic and cultural life of that colony. Constituting about one-tenth to one-fifth of the South Carolina population in the eighteenth century, they furnished a much larger proportion of the distinguished names of that proud community. Among them are such well-known names in American history as Bayard, Dubois, Laurens, Marion, Gaillard. By the end of the colonial period all but one of the French-speaking churches had become English-speaking Episcopalian churches. Indeed their rapid assimilation has been one of "the most remarkable phenomena in the history of American foreign groups."

Another strain of early French influence of a different kind came from the old French establishments at New Orleans, Vincennes, and other communities, the survivals of the French empire in North America. To-

[9]Durham: Duke University Press, 1928.

day the most foreign of all American cities is New Orleans, while the state of Louisiana's legal system is based on the Code Napoléon, rather than the English common law, and its local government on the parish system. The cruel transportation of the French Acadians in 1755 added some six thousand French-speaking people. A large proportion of those who remained made their way to Louisiana where their descendants are still to be found, constituting some fifty thousand of the present population. To this day they have retained their peculiar French customs, dialect, folklore, and folk music.[10]

Of the two to three thousand Jews who were in America at the end of the colonial period, a great majority were of Spanish or Portuguese origin.[11] In 1654 all Jews were expelled from Brazil, and at least twenty-three came directly to the English colonies. At about the same time others arrived from Holland by way of England. The first Jewish settlement in America was in New Amsterdam. At first the position of the Jews there was insecure because of the intolerance of the Dutch Governor Stuyvesant and the opposition of Domine Johann Megapolensis. The Dutch West India Company, however, took a different view. The company was willing to have them remain, and ordered the governor to cease his opposition to them. In 1683 the Duke's Law

[10]Wittke, *op. cit.*, pp. 31-32.
[11]Anita L. Lebeson, *Jewish Pioneers in America* (New York, 1931), pp. 44-45.

allowed the Jews freedom of worship, though a synagogue was not built until 1728.

Another early American Jewish community was in Newport, Rhode Island. By the opening of the Revolution, this community numbered at least sixty families. Smaller Jewish communities were also found in Philadelphia and Charleston, and Jewish peddlers were familiar figures throughout the colonies.[12]

As a general rule the American colonial Jews were of the lower middle class economically, though by the end of the period a few had become wealthy. The majority were either skilled artisans or ordinary craftsmen. In every community where they were permitted to do so, they built synagogues, which became the centers of their social as well as their religious life. As a whole they lived a life apart, and were distrusted. But there are instances of intermarriage between Jews and Christians, and not infrequently Jews became members of Masonic lodges. It is also interesting to note that the colonial Jews differed among themselves in their political views. During the Revolution there were Tories among them, though a great majority were "patriots," and not a few Jews in America today can qualify for membership in the Sons and Daughters of the American Revolution.[13]

The Germans constituted by far the largest number of non-English-speaking people in colonial America. It

[12]The Minute Book of the Newport congregation. See American Jewish Historical Society Publication 33, Vols. XXI and XXVII.
[13]Wittke, op. cit., pp. 39-42.

has been estimated that at the time of the Declaration of Independence one-tenth of the population of the new nation were people of German blood and that one-third of them were living in Pennsylvania. Religion and economics were about equally responsible for the beginning of this great flow of German people to America. William Penn's effective advertising of his great proprietaryship of Pennsylvania, his liberal land policy, and his promise of religious freedom made Pennsylvania their principal New World haven.

It was the Mennonites, a religious body in southern Europe without legal status, who blazed the trail to the New World for the vast numbers of their race who were to follow. Today, it is stated that twenty thousand Mennonites go to church every Sunday in Lancaster County, Pennsylvania. And it is no accident that that county is one of the most prosperous agricultural communities in the United States, if not the most prosperous. Another small persecuted German group, the Dunkers, now known as the Church of the Brethren, soon followed; and these groups, with the Schwenkfelders, largely account for the preservation of what may be termed the Pennsylvania Dutch culture. Today, with the exception of one congregation in London, all the Dunkers in the world outside mission fields are to be found in the United States. As a whole, however, by far the largest number of colonial Germans were those of German Lutheran or German Reformed background, who came largely for economic reasons.

The colonial Germans were for the most part people

of the peasant type, and were more noted for their industry and frugality than for their refinement and education. In fact they pretty generally frowned upon education for the common man, and looked upon it as essentially a church matter. Many colonial Pennsylvania leaders had a poor opinion of the Germans. Franklin on one occasion denounced them as "the most stupid of their nation," while William Smith, the first provost of the University of Pennsylvania, considered them "utterly ignorant." They were slow in organizing schools, and many of them opposed the introduction of public schools in the nineteenth century.

Yet in spite of these facts the colonial Germans made distinct contributions to American culture. In both instrumental and vocal music they were outstanding. In the Moravian communities of Bethlehem and Nazareth church music was more highly developed than anywhere else in the colonies; hymns and litanies made up a large part of their formal worship.[14] Even in Pennsylvania German farmhouses zithers, spinets, and hand organs were not unknown, while organs were fairly common in the German churches in the larger communities. The Pennsylvania Germans also made a distinct artistic contribution, especially in pottery, glassware, and furniture. In the realm of culinary art the colonial Germans also excelled. The Pennsylvania German *hausfrau* was proud of her reputation as a cook. Those who have experienced the delicious fragrance that comes from frying scrapple in a Pennsylvania Ger-

[14]The community of Ephrata was also a music center.

[13]

man farmhouse on a cold frosty morning will, I am sure, acknowledge our debt to the culinary art of the German.

Before the end of the colonial era the Germans had made distinguished contributions in the realms of the higher culture. William Rittenhouse, the first paper manufacturer in America, was a Dunker minister. On his death the mill was carried on by his son Klaas Rittenhouse, also a Dunker preacher. David Rittenhouse, the great-grandson of William, a veritable mathematical genius, was the greatest mathematician and astronomer the colonies produced. He was professor of astronomy and for a time vice-provost of the College of Philadelphia, and succeeded Franklin as president of the American Philosophical Society, the oldest of American learned societies.

Few families in America can equal the Muhlenbergs in the distinction of their contributions. Henry M. Muhlenberg, the founder of the family in America and the father of American Lutheranism, married a daughter of Conrad Weiser, the famous Indian interpreter and the best backwoods diplomat of his time. Of the eleven children of this union, all the sons became Lutheran ministers and most of the daughters married Lutheran ministers. One of the sons, John Peter Gabriel, became one of Washington's most trusted generals, and another, Frederick Augustus Conrad, was the first speaker of the federal House of Representatives.[15]

[15]See sketches of seven members of the Muhlenberg family in the *Dictionary of American Biography*.

Though not "foreigners" in the same sense as the Germans or the Huguenots, the colonial immigrants from Ireland introduced a large element of non-English influence. The total number of Scotch-Irish added to the colonial population by immigration has been estimated at between 150,000 and 200,000. The first North Irish immigrants to America entered by way of New England ports. Though Calvinists and Presbyterians, they were not welcomed by the New England Calvinists, who resented their coming, especially after they had gained a reputation for pugnacity and aggressiveness. Later Philadelphia and the Delaware River ports were the principal places of debarkation and Pennsylvania became their great mecca and distribution center. By the end of the colonial era the Scotch-Irish were to be found in at least five hundred separate communities from Maine on the north to Georgia on the south.[16]

This great Scotch-Irish colonial immigration led to the rapid growth of colonial Presbyterianism, so that by the end of the colonial era the Presbyterians ranked second only to the Congregationalists in the number of their congregations. With their long and proud tradition of an educated ministry the Presbyterians became the principal educators of the early American frontier. The College of New Jersey, established in 1746, the first of the "colonial immigrant" colleges, was the

[16]William Warren Sweet, *Religion on the American Frontier*, Vol. II, *The Presbyterians* (New York, 1936), particularly chap. iii, "Cultural and Educational Influence of the Presbyterians in the Early

principal training center for the Presbyterian ministry, though it was supplemented by a whole group of "Log Colleges" and academies conducted by Presbyterian ministers. In fact many a Presbyterian minister considered himself at least half schoolteacher. From the close of the Revolution to 1840, the Presbyterians were the most important single educational influence in America.[17]

During the period of the great Scotch-Irish immigration there was also a considerable mingling of Scotch Highlanders and Catholic Irish. As might be expected, the Tory element among the revolutionary Presbyterians was confined almost entirely to the Scotch Highlanders.[18] Recent studies by Roman Catholics[19] have tended to overemphasize the Catholic Irish element in revolutionary America, though there is no doubt that there were larger numbers of Catholic Irish than was formerly acknowledged.

West." See also Wittke, *op. cit.*, chap. v, "The Colonial Immigration from Ireland: The Irish and Scotch-Irish."

[17]Donald G. Tewksbury, *The Founding of American Colleges and Universities Before the Civil War with Particular Reference to the Religious Bearing upon the College Movement* (New York, 1932), pp. 55-91.

[18]J. P. MacLean, *A Historical Account of the Settlement of Scotch Highlanders in America prior to the Peace of 1783* (Cleveland, 1900).

[19]By Michael J. O'Brien. The two books that have stressed the Catholic Irish influence in revolutionary America are *A Hidden Phase of American History: Ireland's Part in America's Struggle for Liberty* (New York, 1919), and *The Pioneer Irish in New England* (New York, 1937). See a critical review of the first mentioned book by J. Franklin Jameson in the *American Historical Review*, XXVI (July, 1921), 797-99.

By the beginning of the nineteenth century the large non-English immigration of the eighteenth was far on the way toward assimilation. The principal exceptions were to be found among the Germans, and especially the small clannish sects such as the Mennonites and the Dunkers whose religious principles set them apart from political participation. The assimilation of German Lutherans and German Reform people was likewise retarded by the long continuance of the German language in their services as well as by the widespread use in German communities of "Pennsylvania Dutch," which is "the oldest immigrant language still in daily use in the United States." The work of the German printer Christopher Saur and the German Press at Ephrata; the widespread circulation of German newspapers, almanacs, and books; and the German parochial schools were all elements in the retarding of assimilation and the preservation of Old World customs, superstitions, and folklore.

The fact that an overwhelming proportion of the colonial immigration was of Protestant background largely explains the relative rapidity with which assimilation proceeded. Throughout the colonial period and on into the nineteenth century fear and distrust of Roman Catholicism were widespread, and disability clauses were incorporated in several of the new state constitutions.[20]

[20]Sister Mary Augustana (Ray), *American Opinion of Roman Catholicism in the Eighteenth Century* (New York, 1936), is an elaborate study of anti-Catholic attitudes and activities in the colonial period. See chap. ix, "Making the Constitutions," pp. 350-93.

It might be an interesting exercise to conjecture what would have been the religious complexion of present-day America had the same kind of immigration restrictions been imposed at the beginning of the national period that we now have in the federal statutes. The Immigration Act of 1924, which was passed by an overwhelming majority of both houses of Congress, provides for the limitation of immigrants to 2 per cent of the number of foreign-born of each of the various peoples living in the United States in 1890. If such an act had been in force from 1790 on, it would have meant the exclusion of practically all immigration from southern and eastern Europe as well as the Orient. This would have meant that there would now be no Eastern Orthodox churches in the United States and only a small fraction of the number of Roman Catholics there are now. There would have been relatively few Scandinavians, so that among the Lutherans in the country would have been numbered the people of German origin only. The Roman Catholics would have been almost entirely of Irish and German stock, with only a very small proportion of converts of other racial strains. If such restrictions had been imposed a hundred and fifty years ago we would have been a largely homogeneous people rather than the most polyglot nation of the world. Yet who is there among us who would have had things different from what they are in this respect, in spite of the almost insuperable problems which our population situation poses for us?

IV

The immigration to America during the first three-quarters of the nineteenth century is usually termed the "old immigration." It was largely a movement of the same racial stocks that were already to be found in the United States at the end of the colonial period; namely, Irish, German, English, Scotch, and Scandinavians. With the exception of the Irish this immigration was still predominantly of a Protestant complexion, though it has been estimated that a third of the Germans who came after 1830 were of Catholic background.

The great German tide set in after 1830, and from 1845 to 1860 it became a veritable flood. During this period 1,250,000 Germans arrived. Lovers of the land, generally pretty well supplied with resources, they came west, and their instinct for the soil led them to select fertile farms in the states of the Old Northwest and on into Missouri and Iowa. The skilled workers among them and the intellectuals were attracted to the growing central western cities, and in Cincinnati, Milwaukee, St. Louis, Buffalo, Cleveland, Detroit, Chicago, and numerous smaller cities of the Northwest, German was for a time almost as common a language as English. Indeed there was considerable talk of establishing a separate German state, and Illinois, Wisconsin, and Missouri were considered as possible sites for a Germany in America. Though for three generations their German churches, parochial schools, *Turnvereins*, musical clubs, picnics, and beer gardens kept them apart, these immigrants had no love for the Germany they had left and consequently no desire to return.

Coming to the raw new West they introduced the seeds of artistic appreciation, and their respect for education influenced the rising new state universities. Among them were able leaders, imbued with democratic ideals, of whom Carl Schurz is an example, though by no means an isolated one; there were many others of his kind, men who considered it an honor and a privilege to be American citizens. Many, however, looked upon these newcomers as enemies of the true America, because of their introduction of the Continental Sunday with its accompanying beer drinking and picnic excursions and other Old World practices out of harmony with puritanical ideas and practices.[21]

The last phase of German immigration began about 1870 and continued to the opening of World War I. This immigration outnumbered all others: from 1870 to 1910 3,750,000 Germans arrived. They were to a larger degree industrial workers than the earlier German immigrants had been; and though many took up lands in Kansas, Nebraska, the Dakotas, they more and more moved to the cities where they found employment in factories and in those trades in which Germans excel. Many, if not a majority, of these later Germans came imbued with *der Deutsche Geist* and tended to be contemptuous and critical of everything in their new home.

[21]Samuel P. Orth, *Our Foreigners* (New Haven, 1921), chap. vi, "The Teutonic Tide." See also Wittke, *op. cit.*, chap. ix, "The Germans."

Those who came after 1900 generally refused to be naturalized and considered themselves German rather than American citizens. German propaganda financed from Germany attempted to bring every German church, school, club, and newspaper in America into the service of the new Germany. The great majority of the people of the older German stock, however, were thoroughly out of sympathy with this program of Prussianization.

V

No immigration ever aroused more resentment and fear on the part of the older Americans than the transplanting of half the population of Ireland to America. It was the most poverty-stricken, illiterate, improvident immigration that had ever set foot on American soil. Entirely without resources, the Irish were compelled to settle down in the cities where they landed; and their genius for organization and political manipulation soon gave them control of city governments in many cities along the Atlantic seaboard. By 1860 the total Irish population in the United States was 1,611,304, and since 1820 4,250,000 Irish immigrants have found their way to our shores. They were practically 100 per cent Roman Catholic, and a large percentage remained true to that faith. Today the Roman Catholic church in America is largely manned by the Irish element. The Irish-American has largely retained his anti-English attitude, as Orth points out in *Our Foreigners*.

"Wherever the human touch is the essential of success, there you find the Irish." In not a few great cities half the teachers are Irish; "they are the most successful walking delegates, solicitors, agents, foremen and contractors." Wherever dash, brilliance, cleverness, and emotion are demanded, you will find the Irish. They are numerously represented in the law, the priesthood, politics; journalism and literature attract them. In spite of all their faults and failings, America would not be America without them.

VI

There are today in the United States at least four million people of Scandinavian blood—Swedes, Norwegians, Danes, and Finns. This great exodus from Europe was motivated almost entirely by economic considerations. Coming largely from agricultural countries in the Old World, the Scandinavians tended to become farmers in the New World. In 1930 four-fifths of the American Swedes lived in rural communities. Much the same proportion prevails also among the Norwegians, Danes, and Finns. Practically 100 per cent Lutheran in background, they have transplanted their Lutheranism to America, though in America only a relatively small proportion have actually become communicants of churches. Wentz states that only 30 per cent of the Norwegians, 20 per cent of the Swedes, and 7 per cent of the Danes are communicants of any church.[22] Members of the Lutheran state churches in their homelands,

[22]Abdel R. Wentz, *The Lutheran Church in American History* (Philadelphia, 1923), p. 222. See also George M. Stephenson, *The Religious Aspects of Swedish Immigration* (Minneapolis, 1932).

most of them who remained in the church on coming to America are still Lutherans, though all of the American Scandinavian Lutheran churches have suffered schisms. Thus they have added to the religious complexity of the United States. According to the religious census of 1936 there are at least eight Scandinavian Lutheran churches in America, besides several non-Lutheran Scandinavian religious bodies.

Their industry, honesty, aptitude for agriculture, and instinct for self-government have enabled the Scandinavians to become almost at once valuable members of American society. They took an active part in forming local governmental units in the Dakotas and Minnesota, and it was not long until they had able leaders in state and national affairs, not a few of whom have gained general recognition.[23]

Samuel P. Orth has thus summarized the Scandinavian part in building modern America:

> Without brilliance, producing few leaders, the Norseman represents the rugged commonplace of American life, avoiding the catastrophes of a soaring ambition on the one hand and the pitfalls of a jaded temperamentalism on the other. Bent on self-improvement, he scrupulously patronizes farmers' institutes, high schools, and extension courses, and listens with intelligent patience to lectures that would put an American audience to sleep. This son of the North has greatly buttressed every worthy American institution with the stern traditional virtues of the tiller of the soil. Strength he gives, if not grace, and that at a time when all social institutions are being shaken to their foundations.[24]

[23]K. C. Babcock, *The Scandinavian Element in the United States* (New York, 1914).
[24]*Op. cit.*, p. 159.

VII

The great inundation of immigrant peoples sweeping into the United States after 1880, largely from eastern and southern Europe, is generally characterized as the "new immigration" in contrast to what is called the "old immigration" from northern and western Europe. The new immigrants may also be appropriately designated as the "city builders," since a vast majority of them sought the cities. The mere listing of them fills one almost with dismay at the complexity of the problems which their presence among us causes.[25]

A million eight hundred thousand Czechs; 500,000 Slovaks; 3,400,000 Poles; many thousands of Serbs, Montenegrins, Slovenes, Croats, and Dalmatians (grouped, following World War I, under the name Jugoslavs but in the United States maintaining their separate entities); 750,000 Russians; 500,000 Ukrainians or Ruthenians; 600,000 Hungarians; Bulgarians and Lithuanians, together 600,000; 40,000 Latvians; 5,000,000 Italians; 400,000 Greeks; more than 200,-000 Armenians; 150,000 Portuguese; and 1,000,000 Mexicans; besides Chinese, Japanese, and 4,000,000 Jews from the four corners of the earth: such is the "new immigration."

The "new immigration" added greatly, as did the "old," to the religious diversity of America, and tested to the full, from the beginning, the greatest of our freedoms—religious liberty. The Czechs were divided

[25]Brown and Roucek, *op. cit.*, pp. 236-41.

between Catholics and non-Catholics. Many are un-churched, while freethinkers' organizations are still numerous among them. The Czechs have broken from Catholicism far more than any other Slavic group in America. Lutheranism is relatively strong among American Slovaks, though they have remained Catholic to a larger degree than the Czechs. Numerous American denominations have also been active among both groups. Lithuanians are about 80 per cent Catholic and 10 per cent Lutheran; Latvians are about three-fourths Protestant and about 19 per cent Catholic.

Among the Poles the Roman Catholic church plays the leading role, both religiously and as a social agency. They have retained their Old World religious affiliations more fully than any other group in the "new immigration," though they frequently express opposition to the Irish control of American Catholicism. Hungarians are divided between Catholics and Protestants, with the Protestants probably in the majority. The Hungarian Reformed church, now a part of the Evangelical and Reformed church in America, has the largest number of parishes, though there are also numerous Baptists and Presbyterians. The American Italians have retained to a larger degree their Catholic affiliation, though there has been a considerable drift away from Rome both into Protestant bodies and, to a larger extent, into irreligion.

The "new immigration" brought to America strong Eastern Orthodox elements, represented by the Greeks, the Russians, the Bulgarians, the Ukrainians, the Ru-

manians, and the Serbians, together with a number of
Roman Catholic churches of the Greek rite. Practically
all Greeks in America consider themselves members of
the church, and they represent the largest number
among the Eastern Orthodox bodies. The Russian Orthodox are numerically in second place.

VIII

The groups composing the new immigration have
made varied contributions to our culture. Many, such
as the Poles, the Slovaks, the Russians, and the Italians,
are still engaged principally in unskilled labor. Others,
such as the Greeks, who came as laborers, soon became
proprietors of small business enterprises. Of all the
southern Europeans, they seem to be the most individualistic and aggressive, and will succeed where conditions permit individual effort. The Armenians have
gone into business and into the professions more largely
in proportion to their numbers than others. In all of
our large cities you will find Armenians in the oriental
rug business, in which they have gained an international
reputation. In business, in the professions, in philan-
thropy, and in education and scientific research, the Jews
have made rich contributions.

The Jews, who constitute today one of the major
religious groups in America, are 99 per cent city dwell-
ers. Aside from their religious significance, the Jewish
congregations carry on charitable and social work among
their own people both here and abroad. But their philan-
thropy is by no means limited to the Jewish people. The

work for the Negro carried on by the Rosenwald Foundation is a notable example. Their aid to immigrants has been large and effective, not only in a material way but also in preparing them for citizenship.[26]

Perhaps in no other realm has the contribution of the southern European been more conspicuous than in that of music and art. The Germans among the earlier immigrants really laid the foundation for orchestral music in America when in 1848 the Germania orchestra began to give concerts in New York, Philadelphia, Baltimore, and Boston. In later years the Czechs, Poles, Italians, and Russians came more and more to fill places in orchestras once monopolized by the Germans. In 1930 the 114 members of the New York Philharmonic orchestra included seventy-two naturalized citizens and twelve aliens. Among the naturalized members were twenty-nine Russians, one Spaniard, thirteen Italians, two Austrians, four Hungarians, and ten Germans. Other large city orchestras in the United States are not greatly different in their personnel. In opera, America is equally indebted to the southern Europeans. Their contributions to other forms of American art, while not as large as in music, yet are impressive. This is indicated by the fact that about half the painters listed in Van Dyke's *American Painting and Its Tradition* are of mixed blood.

IX

The story of the peopling of modern America is an amazing one. Any consideration of the complexity of

[26]See *ibid.*, chap. ix, "Jewish Americans," pp. 406-25.

the population of the United States throughout our history naturally gives rise to the question, "Is the United States a real nation?" A nation has been defined as "the political unity of people." How is this political unity to be secured—and do we have such unity in America today?

Is racial unity a necessity for political unity? If so, then the United States is not a nation today, nor can it become a nation until complete amalgamation is secured.

Is unity of language necessary for the achievement of national unity? If so, then we are not a real nation. Today there are more foreign language newspapers published in the United States in proportion to the part of the population which reads them, than in all Europe.

Is unity of religion a necessity for securing national unity? It was once so considered. If it is a necessity then we can never become a nation until we give up the basic freedom of all our freedoms, the freedom of conscience.

The attempt to enforce religious unity has led to untold suffering and persecution in the long past. Such attempts have not been a monopoly of any one religious body. Catholics, Protestants, and Jews have all been guilty, at one time or another, of attempting to maintain religious unity by force. The chief thing these attempts had in common was the injustice, the cruelty, and the suffering which they entailed. If religious unity is a necessity for national unity, then the United States is farther from it than any other nation in the world. According to the last federal religious census there are 256 independent religious bodies in the United States, every one of which, from the smallest to the largest, enjoys equal rights and privileges with the others under the law.

But if we *are* a real nation, what is it that makes us one?

The first absolute necessity in the achievement of nationality is *common experience*. A nation, like an individual, is the product of experience. We are a united people in spite of our differences, because we are agreed about certain great ideas and ideals, one of which is religious freedom. Americans as a whole believe in "living and letting live" religiously. And there is nothing more un-American than for any one religious body even to dream of eventually controlling the religious life of America through the medium of legal restrictions. We have come to this position as a result of our experience.

A second necessity in the achievement of national unity is *common memories*. History has been defined as the memory of a people. Memories of common triumphs to rejoice in, common sorrows and common problems faced. Indeed, common disasters are often more powerful in their influence in creating a feeling of unity than are common joys. It was the half-century of bitter suffering and loss in their long struggle against the Spaniard which welded the Dutch people into a nation.

Third, though we may not be bound together by a long common past, we all believe in a common future, in the building of which we can all have a part.

Recent studies have shown that the real source of

much of our racial hostility is not physical but cultural.[27] The remedy for this, however, is not the obliteration of all cultural differences, but rather the blending of all that is best from all cultures. And no nation in the world has such an opportunity as has ours to achieve this goal.

[27]Montagu, *op. cit.*, esp. chap. x, "Race and Culture."

2

PROTESTANTISM AND DEMOCRACY

Most Anglo-Americans would agree with Aristotle's famous dictum that the good life consists in the achievement of the greatest happiness or well-being of the individuals who compose society. We believe also that democracy has been more successful in achieving this end than has any other form of government.

Democracy strives to achieve the good life through the sovereignty of the same individuals who are not only the beneficiaries of organized society but also the sources of its power. Or to put it in the classic terms of Abraham Lincoln, the good life is achieved through a government "of the people, by the people and for the people."

This, in its simplest terms, is what we mean by democracy. Its purpose is to give to people what they want instead of what the government wants for them. It places supreme value upon the well-being of individuals. Nondemocratic states, by substituting some corporate good such as military glory and territorial expansion for the real interests of the people, have only succeeded in luring them to their own destruction.

Modern democratic ideas had their beginnings in the fifteenth and sixteenth centuries and sprang from a new emphasis upon the supreme worth of the individual which arose out of the Renaissance and Reformation. In a brilliant book on the Renaissance published some years ago, Edward M. Hulme orients his readers by a series of chapters on revivals. These were the revival of learning, the revival of literature, the revival of art, and the revival of trade. But, the author points out, the basic revival of them all, the one out of which all the others came, was the revival of the individual.

During the Medieval age the individual had become submerged. From birth to death the individual's life was dominated by agencies over which he had no control and in the management of whose affairs he had no voice. No individual was able to stand on his own feet or permitted to think his own thoughts. Medieval art, learning, literature, religion, were all circumscribed by rules and regulations which left no place for the expression of individuality.

It was the throwing overboard of these restraints which released the individual and created the Renaissance. But the emphasis upon individuality was not alone a Renaissance emphasis. As Hegel has stated, the whole emphasis of the Reformation was individualistic also. It is through the channel of individuality that all the great beneficent changes in the modern world have taken place. Indeed individuality, the force of separate selfhood, is the most important fact in human life and lies at the heart not only of democracy but also of the Christian gospel.

Although Luther held to no definite political opinions, his great collaborator, Melanchthon, clearly recognized the rights which belong to man as man. These rights are based on the law of nature, which is the law of God. Melanchthon held that no ruler had the right to command anything contrary to that law. In other words, he held that no ruler might violate the inherent rights of man. Thus over against the medieval claim of the divine rights of kings were placed the divine rights of the individual man.

Unfortunately, however, a political situation developed in Germany during Luther's lifetime which made it necessary, for his own safety as well as for that of German Protestantism itself, that the movement come under the protection of the German princes. In consequence, Lutheranism came to be more and more a department of the state. Thus its safety was secured, but at the expense of liberty. It was this historic factor, more than any other single thing, which accounted for the tragic religious situation that prevailed in German Lutheranism under the Nazi regime.

Although Calvin's position on individual rights, as set forth in his *Institutes*, is contradictory and confused, yet the net outcome of his teaching on civil government made for individual rights. His theories of democracy were mutilated by a theocratic bias both in Geneva and in New England, but the theories of individual rights persisted and eventually resulted in the emancipation of the people. It might even be argued, as C. P. Gooch suggests, that the theocratic element protected and fostered the democratic principle in an age when creed was the dominant factor of national life. As the theocratic spirit declined, the popular basis of government came more and more clearly into view.

Gooch, in his *History of Democratic Ideas in the Seventeenth Century*, thus summarizes the contribution made by the Reformation to modern democracy: "Modern democracy is the child of the Reformation, not of the Reformers." Modern democracy owes to the Reformation the enunciation of two basic intellectual principles: the first, the right of free inquiry; the second, the priesthood of all believers. "The first led to liberty; the second, to equality."

From the Reformation there emerged two distinct types of Protestantism, which may be characterized respectively as right-wing and left-wing. The first included all those Protestant churches which were established by law in all the lands in western Europe where Protestantism gained the upper hand. Thus Lutheranism was established by law in the German states and in the Scandinavian countries. The Church of England, the Reformed churches of the Continent, and the Presbyterian church of Scotland all were right-wing bodies and all of them were established by law. In the various countries these established bodies became the only legal religions. They also were confessional churches; that is, they formulated and adopted elaborate confessions of faith. In this respect they had much in common with Roman Catholic doctrines, though they discarded the penitential system of medieval Catholicism. In other words, right-wing Protestantism did not break entirely with the past, but preserved such attitudes and practices in common with medieval Christianity as enforced uniformity to a state religion and the denial of the right of private judgment. Thus what the leading reformers proclaimed in theory in regard to individual rights was actually denied in practice by the Protestant state churches.

Because of the prominence of such leaders as Calvin, Luther, Zwingli, and Cranmer, most well-informed people think of the Reformation almost exclusively in terms of its right-wing phase and of the great Protestant state churches. Historians likewise have stressed the right-wing Protestant movements. In fact, only in recent years has there been any serious attempt to do full justice to the left-wing phase of the Protestant revolt.

The left-wing phase of the Reformation began among the peasants of Germany and eventually spread into all Protestant lands in the face of bitter persecution. As the name implies, it was a radical movement which not only threw overboard the penitential system of medieval Roman Catholicism, but rejected formal creeds and placed principal stress upon Christianity as a life rather than upon Christianity as a body of doctrine or as an institution.

Its leadership came from among the common people. It rejected state churches and repudiated the right of civil authority to interfere in any way in matters of conscience. In the long run, as Professor Carlton J. H. Hayes has pointed out, these radical or left-wing Protestant groups were to prove far more characteristic of Protestantism than either Luther or Calvin, because in their total impact they substituted "individualistic for collective Christianity."

In other words, what Luther and Calvin held in theory only, these left-wing groups put into practice. All the great ideas for which democracy stands today— individual rights, freedom of conscience, freedom of speech, freedom of assembly and of the press, the inherent right of self-government, and the separation of the church and state—are concepts which have come directly out of the left-wing phase of the Reformation and only indirectly out of its right-wing phase.

Democracy had its principal development where the political philosophy of individual rights had the freest opportunity to take root. And that, naturally, was in those nations where Protestantism early gained dominance. Thus democracy had its most favorable opportunity in the Protestant states of Europe—in Holland, in Switzerland, in England and Scotland, and in the Scandinavian states. It lagged in Germany because of the political situation which retarded the putting into practice of the cardinal principles of the Reformation. In France, in Italy, and in other parts of Europe the development of democratic ideas was delayed until political and social revolution had swept away the old controls. Consequently, in these lands democracy did not have as favorable a basis or as normal a development as it enjoyed in those lands where the philosophy of individual rights was founded upon Protestant ideals and ideas.

In sixteenth- and seventeenth-century Europe left-wing Protestantism was everywhere under a legal ban; in the New World, on the other hand, it was to find a political and social soil suitable for its growth and development. There it came to full fruition.

Although right-wing Protestantism was the first to be transplanted to the American colonies, its early power resulting in the establishment of state churches in nine of the colonies, by the end of the colonial period left-wing religious ideas had come to prevail. This change in the religious situation in eighteenth-century America was due to four main factors.

The first was the great immigration which swept into the colonies in the eighteenth century and raised the population from 250,000 in 1690 to 2,500,000 by the opening of the American Revolution. This astonishing increase was due largely to non-English immigration, consisting of Germans, French Huguenots, Scotch-Irish, Scotch, and Quakers, all of them coming to obtain economic advantages, but also to escape religious disabilities imposed by state churches in their homelands.

A second factor which fostered left-wing Protestantism in America was the great colonial revivals which swept like a tidal wave over the land regardless of colonial boundaries. In all the revivals, theologies were reduced to a few simple principles which the common man could comprehend. The emphasis was upon the personal rather than upon the institutional, upon life

rather than upon creed. The net result was a great increase in the number of dissenters, and by the end of the
colonial period dissenters were in the majority everywhere except in New England, where Congregationalism—the state religion—remained dominant.

A third influence which strengthened left-wing ideas
was the total effect of pioneering upon ideas and attitudes. The pioneer of necessity becomes a self-reliant
individualist, inclined to go his own way with little regard for the traditional ways of doing things. In many
instances his major purpose in migrating from the Old
World to the New was to escape the social inequalities and the depressing conventions of the Old World
communities. Thus the natural inclination of the pioneer was to become left-wing in his religious ideas,
stressing the practical rather than the theoretical, the
personal rather than the institutional. Since the great
majority were out of touch with organized religion,
they were forced to be self-dependent in their religious
life, finding leadership among men of their own kind
rather than among the professionally trained ministry.

While the common man in eighteenth-century colonial America was becoming increasingly left-wing in his
religious views as a consequence of the new immigration, of the revivals, and of pioneering, many of the
political leaders were reaching the same position
through quite a different set of influences. The writings
of John Locke, who became the American philosopher
par excellence of the eighteenth century, constituted one
of these influences. In his treatises on *Government* and

on *The Reasonableness of Christianity as Delivered in the Scriptures* and his letters on *Toleration*, Locke argued for the separation of church and state, contending that religion was primarily a personal concern and that liberty of conscience was every man's right.

John Locke was largely responsible for passing on these left-wing Protestant ideas to Thomas Jefferson, James Madison, and others of our constitutional fathers. They, in turn, were responsible for writing them into the fundamental law of the land.

Thus the great basic freedoms which we enjoy in the Anglo-American lands — religious liberty, freedom of speech, freedom of the press, and the right of self-government—are to a large degree Protestant accomplishments. And if they are to be retained, they must be preserved by a united and intelligent Protestantism.

3

NATURAL RELIGION AND RELIGIOUS LIBERTY

THE tree of religious freedom which came to something like full fruition in America in the latter part of the eighteenth century has many and varied roots. There were certain practical matters, such as the necessity of securing colonists for the great unpeopled wilderness that was colonial America, which helped to create an environment favorable to religious freedom. There were Lord Baltimore's and Roger Williams' experiments in religious freedom in Maryland and Rhode Island, and the Quaker influence in New Jersey, Pennsylvania, and Delaware, which had a far-reaching effect in helping to prove that religious liberty was workable. Because the American colonies became a refuge for people persecuted for conscience from all western Europe, a great variety of religious minority groups came to these shores; their presence tended, more and more, to create a feeling of general toleration throughout colonial society. Then, there was the growing influence of the merchant class on the lookout for new markets. Writing to the President of the Council of Virginia in 1750, the Lords of Trade in London stated: "... as Toleration and a free Exercise of Religion is so valuable a branch of true liberty, and so essential to the enriching and improving of a Trading Nation, it should ever be held sacred in his Majesty's Colonies."[1]

The colonial revivals, which increased greatly the number of dissenters, especially in those colonies where there were established churches, were still another significant factor. The rapid growth of the Baptists, for whom emphasis upon the complete separation of church and state was the first and most important principle, has especial importance.[2]

John Dewey[3] has suggested that certain ideas flourish when they answer a need and tend to wane when that need is no longer felt. This is well illustrated in the wide currency given certain ideas relative to church-state relationship in eighteenth-century America. These philosophical concepts helped to achieve the separation of church and state, and won wide acceptance throughout the eighteenth century, even outside the circles of so-

[1]William Stevens Perry, *Historical Collections Relating to the American Colonial Church*, Vol. I: *Virginia* (Hartford, 1870), pp. 378-81.

[2]For a discussion of the part taken by the Baptists in the struggle for separation of church and state in New England and Virginia, see: Jacob C. Meyer, *Church and State in Massachusetts, 1740-1833* (Cleveland, 1930); W. T. Thom, *The Struggle for Religious Freedom in Virginia: The Baptists* (Baltimore, 1900); and E. F. Humphrey, *Nationalism and Religion in America* (Boston, 1924).

[3]Dewey holds that thinking can best be explained in terms of its functional relationships to human problems and needs. See John Dewey, *Logic: The Theory of Inquiry* (New York, 1938), esp. chap. iii, "The Existential Matrix of Inquiry: Cultural." Also, *The Philosophy of John Dewey*, ed. Joseph Ratner (New York, 1928), p. 518: "The philosopher has received his problem from the world of action." See also Merle Curti, "The Great Mr. Locke, America's Philosopher, 1783-1861," *Huntington Library Bulletin* No. 11 (April, 1937), pp. 107-51.

called liberals, because they tended to jibe in certain particulars with the practical kind of liberalism which was developing among the common people. It was the synchronizing of these various factors which made possible the writing of Jefferson's Act for the Establishment of Religious Liberty in Virginia and the first amendment to the Constitution of the United States.

II

The thinking of leading eighteenth-century Americans, in a variety of fields, was influenced by the work of John Locke. Exalting reason as the basis of human society, Locke found many enthusiastic disciples throughout the length and breadth of colonial America. His writings were not confined to any one phase of philosophical interest—he wrote convincingly and with clarity upon education, religion and theology, mental philosophy, and political and economic theory.

When John Locke wrote his *Two Treatises of Government* in 1690, he was primarily concerned with producing arguments to justify the Glorious Revolution of 1688.[4] But in seeking justification for the seizure of power by Parliament and for the overthrow of King James he unwittingly was furnishing the principal arguments for American resistance to British authority three generations later. The basic argument was that planted deeply in the hearts of all men is a law of

[4]For a concise recent statement of Locke's influence in revolutionary America see John C. Miller, *Origins of the American Revolution* (Boston, 1943), pp. 167-76.

[42]

nature, which is "God's law," and under this law men enjoy certain "natural rights." When in the course of time it became necessary to form governments with authority over individuals, man surrendered some of his "natural rights," but never all of them, and governments thus formed were as a consequence given only limited powers. Even in a highly organized society the laws of nature were still operative, and governments must respect the laws of nature or forfeit the right to continue. In other words, the law of nature placed limitations upon governments, beyond which they had no power to go.

That these ideas had wide popularity in prerevolutionary America is indicated by the fact that "natural law" and "natural rights" constituted the theme of many a New England election sermon.[5] This law, the law of nature, said Jonathan Mayhew in a sermon preached in Boston in 1754, God has planted deep in the heart of man, "written as with a pen of iron and the point of a diamond." The law of nature is, of course, an unwritten law, though supplemented by the Old and New Testaments, which help make it clear and are not out of harmony with it. This law of nature is discernible through reason and the application of common sense.

In his *The Reasonableness of Christianity as Delivered in the Scriptures,* which appeared in 1695, Locke tells his readers that he has betaken himself "to the

[5]Alice M. Baldwin, *The New England Clergy and the American Revolution* (Durham, 1928), chap. ii.

sole reading of the Scriptures . . . for the understanding of the Christian Religion, and has dismissed all systems of divinity as inconsistent and unsatisfactory."[6] Though, he states, the works of nature give sufficient evidence of a deity, yet through false teaching and foolish and absurd rites instituted by priests in order "to secure their empire," reason has been excluded from religion. Though the rational and thinking part of mankind are able to find God when they seek him through reason and nature, yet reason, speaking ever so clearly to the wise and virtuous, "had never authority enough to prevail on the multitude"; hence the necessity of revelation.

In sending Christ into the world to make the way of salvation so plain and clear that even the humble and unlettered could understand, "the all-merciful God seems to have . . . consulted the poor of this world, and the bulk of mankind."[7] Pursuing this idea further, Locke continued:

The writers and wranglers in religion fill it with niceties, and dress it up with notions, which they make necessary and fundamental parts of it; as if there were no way into the church, but through the academy or lyceum. The greatest part of mankind have not leisure for learning and logick, and superfine distinctions of the schools. Where the hand is used to the plough and the spade, the head is seldom elevated to sublime notions, or exercised in mysterious reasoning. It is well if men of that rank (to say nothing of the other sex) can comprehend plain propositions, and a short reasoning about things familiar to their minds, and nearly allied to their daily experience.

[6]John Locke, *The Reasonableness of Christianity as Delivered in the Scriptures.* In *The Works of John Locke in Nine Volumes* (12th ed., London, 1824), VI, 135-36; 157-58.
[7]*Ibid.*, p. 157.

Go beyond this, and you amaze the greatest part of mankind; and may as well talk Arabick to a poor day-labourer, as the notions and language that the books and disputes of religion are filled with. . . .

Christ, he states, stresses the fact that the poor had the gospel preached to them: "And if the poor had the gospel preached to them, it was, without doubt, such a gospel as the poor could understand; plain and intelligible; and so it was, as we have seen, in the preachings of Christ and his apostles."[8]

Of the many writings of John Locke which were widely known in America none had greater vogue or exercised larger influence than his four letters on toleration.[9] A summary of the salient passages from these notable essays will indicate clearly their significance for church-state relationships in eighteenth-century America.

In his first letter Locke states:

I esteem it above all things necessary to distinguish exactly the business of civil government from that of religion, and to settle the just bounds that lie between the one and the other. If this be not done, there can be no end put to the controversies that will be always arising between those that have, or at least pretend to have, on the one side, a concernment for the interest of men's souls, and on the other side, a care of the commonwealth.[10]

Note the suspicion of the sincerity of the clergy implied in the words "or at least pretend to have . . . a concern-

[8]*Ibid.*, p. 158.

[9]John Locke's first letter on toleration was published in Latin under the title *Epistola de Tolerantia* in March, 1689. His second letter on toleration appeared in October, 1690, the third in 1692, and the fourth in 1706.

[10]John Locke, *Treatise of Civil Government and A Letter Concerning Toleration*, ed. Charles L. Sherman (New York, 1937), p. 171.

ment for the interest of men's souls." He defines the commonwealth as "a society of men constituted only for the procuring, the preserving, and the advancing their own civil interests." The power of civil government is confined to "the things of this world, and has nothing to do with the world to come." "No man can, if he would, conform his faith to the dictates of another. All the life and power of true religion consists in the inward and full persuasion of the mind; and faith is not faith without believing."[11]

The church Locke defines as "a voluntary society of men, joining themselves together of their own accord, in order to the publick worshipping of God, in such a manner as they may judge acceptable to him, and effectual to the salvation of their souls." It is a society completely voluntary and free. Though he considered himself a good Anglican, he nevertheless denies the contention that a church's claim to being a "true church" is dependent upon its having bishops and presbyters with authority derived from the apostles and continued down to the present by an uninterrupted succession. Those who so contend he challenges to show where such an edict has been imposed by Christ. Nor can he find in any of the books of the New Testament any statement which would give the Church of Christ the right or authority to persecute others, "and force [them] by fire and sword, to embrace her faith and doctrine."

[11]*Ibid.*, pp. 172, 173, 175. Charles Chauncy nearly a hundred years later expressed the same thought in words strikingly similar: "There can't be faith where there is not the assent of the mind." *Body of Divinity: Twelve Sermons* (Boston, 1765), p. 83.

Though he acknowledges the right of a church to excommunicate members, he states that it does not thereby deprive the one excommunicated "of those civil goods that he formerly possessed," and it has no "right of jurisdiction over those that are not joined with it."[12] Nor is it the business of religion for one private person to prejudice another person in his civil enjoyments because he is of another church or religion.

In discussing orthodoxy, he states that "every church is orthodox to itself," although to others it may seem erroneous or heretical. There is no judge on earth who can judge between churches about the truth of their doctrines, or as to the purity of their worship. A controversy that arises between churches over such matters "is on both sides equal," and the only decision possible must come from the supreme Judge of all men. The only right way, he urges, to propagate truth is "by strong usage." He adds, "Fire and sword are not proper instruments wherewith to convince men's minds of error, and inform them of truth." Men are free from all dominion over one another in matters of religion.

To Locke religion was primarily a personal concern, and he held that no one can be saved by a religion that he distrusts, or by a worship which he abhors. For an unbeliever "to take up an outward show of another man's profession" is all in vain. "Faith only, and inward sincerity, are the things that procure acceptance with God." No magistrate has the power to enforce by law the use of any rites or ceremonies in the worship of

[12]*Ibid.*, pp. 175, 176, 179, 180, 181.

God, nor has he power to forbid the use of such rites and ceremonies as are approved and practiced by the church. Yet he does have the power to forbid those things in the ceremonies and rites of the churches which are prejudicial to the commonweal of the people. Neither pagans nor any dissenting body of Christians, with any right, may be deprived of their worldly goods by the predominating faction of a court church; nor are any civil rights to be either changed or violated upon account of religion.[18]

Like Roger Williams, Locke held that there was absolutely no such thing under the gospel as a Christian state. Christ, he stated, instituted no commonwealth and prescribed for his followers no new or peculiar form of government; nor did he put the sword in any magistrate's hand with commission to use it in forcing any man to forsake his own religion and receive his. The business of law is not to impose speculative opinions and articles of faith on any church. It is not the business of laws to provide for the truth of opinions, but rather for the security of the commonwealth. Truth, he says, will do well enough if left alone to shift for herself. Liberty of conscience is every man's natural right, equally belonging to dissenters, and nobody ought to be compelled in matters of religion either by law or by force.[14]

[18]*Ibid.*, pp. 192, 193, 197-98, 201.

[14]Many of these ideas are found stated in Roger Williams' *Bloudy Tenent of Persecution* and in his *Bloudy Tenent of Persecution yet more Bloudy* and had been actually put into operation in Rhode Island. For a brief discussion of Williams' position see Sweet, *Religion in Colonial America*, pp. 124-27. Locke, *op. cit.*, pp. 204, 205, 213.

Locke's toleration, however, did not extend to Roman Catholics, since he argued that their first allegiance was to the Pope and that therefore their teaching undermined the power of civil government in its rightful realm. Also, since Catholics did not believe in toleration of others, toleration should not be extended to them. Nor would he extend toleration to infidels, since covenants and oaths, which, he states, are "the bonds of human society," have no hold upon them. Taking away God, even in thought, dissolves all. Yet he would not exclude Mohammedans, pagans, or Jews from civil rights because of their religion, for the commonwealth embraces all men that are honest, peaceable, and industrious. It is not the diversity of opinion, he contends, but rather the refusal of toleration to those that are of different opinions, "that has produced all the bustles and wars that have been in the Christian world because of religion."[15]

And, finally, he insists that every man should have the inherent right to enjoy the same rights that are granted to others. "Is it permitted to worship God in the Roman manner? Let it be permitted to do it in the Geneva form also. Is it permitted to speak Latin in the market-place? Let those that have a mind to it, be permitted to do it also in the church. Is it lawful for any man in his own house to kneel, stand, sit, or use any other posture; and to clothe himself in white or black, in short or in long garments? . . . Whatsoever things are left free by law in the common occasions of life, let

[15]Locke, *op. cit.*, pp. 218, 219.

them remain free unto every church in divine worship."
And finally, no ecclesiastical authority, "whether admin-
istered by the hands of a single person, or many, has
any jurisdiction in things civil, nor any manner or power
of compulsion, nor any thing at all to do with riches
and revenues."[16]

Locke's views on church-state relationships are of
special significance because he was undoubtedly the
father of liberal opinion in eighteenth-century America,
and because he, more than any other, was responsible
for making nature, intuition, and common sense popular
and familiar colonial ideas. Others, of course, made
their contributions, but it was from John Locke particularly that the streams of this type of influence proceeded. Perhaps next in importance to Locke, at least
toward the end of the eighteenth century, in shaping
American liberal opinion was Joseph Priestley, whose
prolific writings on scientific, historical, and religious
subjects were increasingly well known as the eighteenth
century neared its close.

Just previous to the opening of the Revolutionary
War Priestley published in London *An Essay on the
First Principles of Government, and on the Nature of
Political, Civil and Religious Freedom.*[17] He advocates
a broader toleration than did Locke, since he would ex-

[16]*Ibid.*, p. 117.
[17]Joseph Priestley, *An Essay on the First Principles of Government,
and on the Nature of Political, Civil and Religious Freedom, includ-
ing Remarks on Dr. Browne's Code of Education, and on Dr. Balguy's
Sermon on Church Authority* (2nd ed.; London, 1771).
Priestley's astonishing output is at least partly explained by his easy

tend it even to Catholics. He calls attention to the fact
that those nations which have had the largest degree of
toleration have become the most prosperous. He cites
Holland as an example in Europe, and Pennsylvania in
America; both have prospered "in consequence of giv-
ing more liberty in matters of religion." Though not
advocating disestablishment immediately "as too haz-
ardous an experiment," he does propose immediate religious reforms in England, among them the elimination of thirty-eight of the Thirty-nine Articles of
Religion, leaving only the one calling for belief solely
"in the religion of Jesus Christ, as it is set forth in the
New Testament." He also urges that "the system of
toleration be completely carried into execution" in
which every citizen shall have the right to belong to any
church he pleases, without being deprived of any of his
civil rights.[18]

Addressing young men in his Preface to his *Institutes
of Natural and Revealed Religion,* Priestley urges them
to

submit to those who are invested with the supreme power in your
country, and your lawful civil magistrates; but if they would prescribe to you in matters of faith, say that you have but one Father in
heaven, even God, and one Master, even Christ, and stand fast in the
liberty with which he has made you free. Respect a Parliamentary

method of adapting the works of others to his own use. This, however, was a common practice in the eighteenth century, and John
Wesley's literary productivity may be largely explained in the same
way. See I. Woodbridge Riley, *American Philosophies: The Early
Schools* (New York, 1907), pp. 397 ff.

[18]Priestley, *op. cit.,* pp. 130, 198, 200.

king, and cheerfully pay all parliamentary taxes; but have nothing to do with a parliamentary religion, or a parliamentary God.[19]

An avowed Unitarian,[20] Priestley was an insatiable enemy of doctrines—particularly those of transubstantiation, the objective atonement, and the Trinity—and the elaborate Roman Catholic and Anglican hierarchy, which he considered corruptions of the Christianity of Jesus and base frauds perpetrated upon the people. The book of Priestley's which perhaps had the largest vogue in America was his *History of the Corruptions of Christianity* in two volumes, which he considered the most valuable of all his many works, and which Jefferson looked upon as required reading in the education of the young away from narrow orthodoxy.[21] Here Priestley traces through the Christian centuries the gradual evolution of the build-up of Christian doctrine and the development of the elaborate machinery of the church, all designed, he contended, to hold the common people in subjection for the purpose of their exploitation. The views which he expressed came to be widely held in America, not only among the so-called liberals, but among the common people as well.

[19] Joseph Priestley, *Institutes of Natural and Revealed Religion* (London, 1794), pp. iv-v. The language of the above quotation was used by Lord Wharton in the debate on the Act of William and Mary concerning the doctrine of the Trinity.

[20] Joseph Priestley, *Unitarianism Explained and Defended in a Discourse delivered in Philadelphia, 1796* (Philadelphia, 1796).

[21] Jefferson's dependence upon Priestley constituted the groundwork of his creed. H. S. Randall, *Life of Thomas Jefferson* (New York, 1858), Vol. III, chap. xiv.

III

Here we have before us the pattern of liberal thought regarding church-state relationships which came more and more to prevail in eighteenth-century colonial America. John Locke, and to a lesser degree Joseph Priestley and others of the same school, furnished the American revolutionary fathers not only the political philosophy which underlay their attitude toward the mother-country, but also the religious philosophy which determined their attitude toward the church and its relations to the state.

Two points of view in regard to natural religion were to be found among eighteeenth-century American liberals. The first, which may be identified as full-fledged deism, relied solely upon nature for knowledge of God, insisted that natural laws are themselves moral laws, and rejected revelation entirely, not only as unnecessary, but as fraud, perpetrated to deceive. It also rejected the church, since it based its authority on revelation and justified its existence thereby. A second type reconciled natural and revealed religion and bolstered revelation with arguments from nature. Both emphasized reason and common sense, and both were critical of the church and especially hostile to the idea of established churches. Thomas Paine and Ethan Allen are the best-known American representatives of the first type, while Thomas Jefferson, John Adams, Benjamin Franklin, and the relatively large number of southern liberals are representative of the milder type.

The eighteenth-century southern planter aristocracy, especially in Virginia, presented some strange paradoxes. The planters had patrician tastes and yet held liberal views on religion and politics. They were large slave-owners and at the same time were critical of the institution of slavery, looked forward to its abolishment, and considered it a curse to the master as well as to the slave. A few of them, of whom John Randolph, especially in his earlier years, is an example, were disciples of Voltaire and the French deists and were openly hostile to the Christian religion. Most of them, however, were disciples of Locke and Priestley and did not wholly discard the Bible as revelation, but emphasized the worship of the Supreme Being who ruled the universe by natural laws. "Reason and nature were the two shibboleths" which they applied to religion,[22] just as their New England contemporaries were applying the same shibboleths to government.

Thomas Jefferson has given fuller expression to the liberal attitudes on church-state relationships than has any other of the American natural religionists, and it is not difficult to trace the influence of Locke and Priestley upon his thought. In the notes which he prepared for the debate in the Virginia Assembly on the bill of 1779 to establish religious freedom, he states:

[22]Clement Eaton, *Freedom of Thought in the Old South* (Durham, 1940), chap. i, "Aristocrats with Liberal Views," pp. 3-31. Benjamin F. Wright, Jr., *American Interpretations of Natural Law* (Cambridge, 1931), chaps. ii and iii. Also Louis B. Wright, *The First Gentlemen of Virginia* (San Marino: Huntington Library, 1940).

The care of every man's soul belongs to himself. But what if he neglect the care of it? Well what if he neglect the care of his health or estate, which more nearly relate to the state. Will the magistrate make a law that he shall not be poor or sick? Laws provide against injury from others; but not from ourselves. God himself will not save men against their wills. . . . No man has power to save men against their wills. . . .No man has *power* to let another prescribe his faith. Faith is not faith without believing. . . . I may grow rich by art I am compelled to follow, I may recover health by medicines I am compelled to take . . . but I cannot be saved by a worship I disbelieve.[23]

Jefferson's definition of the church is almost word for word that of John Locke:

. . . a *voluntary* society of men, joining themselves together of their own accord, in order to the public worshipping of God in such a manner as they judge acceptable to him and effectual to the salvation of their souls. It is *voluntary* because no man is *by nature* bound to any church. If he find anything wrong in it, he should be as free to go out as he was to come in.[24]

He considered an established church clergy "purveyors of religious intolerance," who "by getting themselves established by law, and ingrafted into the machine of government, has been a very formidable engine against the civil and religious rights of man."[25] He held that the right of an individual to any religious belief was one of his inalienable rights, and with it no government had any justification to interfere. In a letter written in 1815 to the Rev. Charles Clay, formerly rector of St. Anne's Parish, in Albemarle County, Virginia, of which Jefferson nominally was a vestryman, are these flaming words:

[23]*Writings of Thomas Jefferson*, ed. P. L. Ford, II, 99 ff.
[24]*Ibid.*, II, 101.
[25]*Ibid.*, III, 455.

I abuse the priests, indeed, who have so much abused the pure and holy doctrines of their Master, and who have laid me under no obligations of reticence as to the tricks of their trade. The genuine system of Jesus, and the artificial structures they have erected, to make them the instruments of wealth, power, and preëminence to themselves, are as distinct things in my view as light and darkness; and while I have classed them with soothsayers and necromancers, I place Him among the greatest reformers of morals, and scourges of priest-craft that have ever existed.[26]

Again and again in his letters and other writings he returned to the same theme. Christianity, he stated, "when divested of the rags" in which a scheming priesthood "have enveloped it, and brought to the original purity and simplicity of its benevolent institutor, is a religion of all others most friendly to liberty, science, and the freest expansion of the human mind."[27] On another occasion he wrote that they had called him "atheist, deist, or devil" because he had advocated "freedom from their religious dictations"; but he continues, "I have ever thought religion a concern purely between our God and our consciences, for which we were accountable to Him, and not to the priests." As for himself, he says, "I never told my own religion, nor scrutinized that of another. I never attempted to make a convert, nor wished to change another's creed. I have ever judged of the religion of others by their lives. . . . For it is in our lives, and not from our words, that our religion must be read. By the same test the world must

[26]Thomas Jefferson to Rev. Charles Clay, January 29, 1815, from Monticello. *The Writings of Thomas Jefferson*, ed. Andrew A. Lipscomb (Washington, 1905), XIV, 233.
[27]Jefferson to Moses Robinson, March 23, 1801. *Ibid.*, X, 237.

judge me." This, however, he says, "does not satisfy the priesthood."

> They must have a positive, a declared assent to all their interested absurdities. My opinion is that there would never have been an infidel, if there had never been a priest. The artificial structures they have built on the purest of all moral systems, for the purpose of deriving from it pence and power, revolt those who think for themselves, and who read in that system only what is really there.[28]

The simple principles of Christianity did not require a priesthood to explain them. But in order to make necessary a numerous "priesthood," these principles have been sophisticated, ramified, split into hairs, and the texts twisted, until the divine morality of Jesus has been covered with mysteries which require a priesthood to explain them.[29]

James Madison, whose leadership in the struggle for the separation of church and state in Virginia was at least as important as was that of Jefferson, was not so outspoken in his religious views. He did indicate, however, on several occasions that his thought was influenced by the liberal ideas current at the time. Perhaps the years he had spent at the College of New Jersey under the influence of John Witherspoon had given him a more wholesome respect for theological learning than Jefferson possessed. But he has left us in no doubt as to his stand on church-state relationships. He advocated a complete separation between ecclesiastical and civil matters and held that there was not a shadow of

[28] Jefferson to Mrs. M. Harrison Smith, August 6, 1816. *Ibid.*, XV, 60.

[29] Jefferson to Elbridge Gerry, March 29, 1801. *Ibid.*, X, 254.

right on the part of government to intermingle with religion unless it trespass on private rights and public peace. "Its least interference with it," he stated, "would be a most flagrant usurpation." He held that both religion and government would remain purer "the less they mixed together." The great multiplicity of sects which pervades America he considered "the best security for religious liberty. For where there is such a variety . . . there cannot be a majority of any one sect to oppress and persecute the rest." "Religious bondage," he stated in a letter written in 1774, "shackles and debilitates the mind, and unfits it for every noble enterprise, every expanded prospect."[30]

George Mason, another Virginian prominent in the struggle for the separation of church and state, who was the author of the Virginia Bill of Rights and probably drafted Virginia's first constitution, was a liberal in his religious views. He held that religion was simply the duty man owed to his Creator and that it was to be discharged by each individual as reason and conviction dictated. Though an Anglican and vestryman, he desired nevertheless to see the Anglican church placed on an equal footing with others.[31]

[30]*Writings of James Madison*, ed. Gaillard Hunt (New York: G. P. Putnam's Sons, 1900), V, 176; I, 24. James Madison to William Bradford, Jr., April 1, 1774.

[31]For Mason's part in drawing up the Bill of Rights and the Constitution see H. J. Eckenrode, *Separation of Church and State in Virginia* (Richmond, 1910), pp. 43 ff. See also Herbert M. Morais, *Deism in Eighteenth Century America* (New York, 1934), pp. 114, 115.

All sorts of conflicting claims have been made in regard to George Washington's religion. The freethinkers have claimed him; he has often been classed as a deist, this claim being based on the facts that in his writings he most frequently spoke of the Supreme Being in deistic rather than in biblical terms, most often using the term "Providence" rather than the term "God"; that he did not kneel in prayer or take the sacrament when he attended the church services, nor ask for a clergyman to attend him on his deathbed. On the other hand, it has been pointed out that he manifested high religious motives in his national leadership; that he attended church regularly and was a vestryman; that in his Farewell Address and in his numerous addresses to religious bodies he always spoke respectfully of religion and desired it to continue as a vital force in the life of the new nation, and expressed conviction that religion and morality were "essential pillars of civil society."[32] Though it is impossible to determine definitely Washington's religious position, there can be no reasonable doubt that he was in full sympathy with the ideas current among his class concerning the application of reason and common sense to religion.

IV

To what extent the views of the natural religionists of both types were accepted by the common man must

[32]Morais, *op. cit.*, pp. 113, 114. See *George Washington, The Christian* (U. S. George Washington Bicentennial Commission, A. B. Hart, ed.), Washington, 1931.

be largely a matter of conjecture. If one is to judge the extent of their acceptance by the circulation of the post-revolutionary writings of Thomas Paine, they must have had wide vogue among the masses. The acceptance of deism among the college students of the time is fully attested by contemporaries.[33] The election of Thomas Jefferson to the presidency in 1800 is a further indication that his liberal religious views and the leadership he had exerted in the struggle for the separation of church and state were elements in his popularity among the mass of the voters. Those who made the most vicious attacks upon Jefferson were the spokesmen of the privileged religious bodies, while the revivalistic groups and the dissenting elements were pretty generally Jeffersonian in thir political ideas. This was true not only in the South and in the new West, but even in New England.[34] The reason for the support of Jefferson's party by the rapidly growing revivalistic and popular religious bodies becomes clear when a comparison is made between their basic ideas and those held by the intellectual liberals.

In the first place, both agreed on the concept of religion as primarily a concern between God and man. The great mass of the people who had been touched in the

[33]G. Adolph Koch, *Republican Religion: The American Revolution and the Cult of Reason* (New York, 1933), pp. 240-43.

[34]William A. Robinson, *Jeffersonian Democracy in New England* (New Haven, 1916), chap. vii, "Republicanism and Religious Liberty."

Richard Purcell, *Connecticut in Transition, 1775-1818* (Washington, 1918).

great revivals thought of religion as primarily an inner experience. To them it was basically a personal affair rather than an institutional matter. Again and again the personal nature of religion is stressed by Locke, Priestley, Jefferson, Madison, and Mason. The revivalistic dissenters well understood what Jefferson meant when he said, "I am a sect by myself," and Thomas Paine when he stated, "My mind is my church." Society in eighteenth-century America was dominantly individualistic. And religion to make any appeal to an individualistic society must make its chief concern the personal problems and needs of the common man and stress the fact that salvation is a personal matter dependent upon individual decisions.

In the second place, both the liberals and the popular religious bodies emphasized the simplicity of the teachings of Jesus. Madison and Jefferson on numerous occasions expressed sympathy for and gave support to the Virginia Baptist farmer-preachers in their struggle for their right to preach what they termed "the simple gospel." The protagonists of natural religion continually advocated the throwing overboard of the dogmatic accumulations of the centuries and a return to the simple and easily understood teachings of Jesus. In this they jibed exactly with the general frontier emphasis. Everywhere among the common people common sense in religion found wide acceptance and popular acclaim.

Third, there was agreement also between the liberals and the popular masses on anticlericalism. The idea that the Established Church clergy were grafters upon the body politic was widely held among the dissenting groups and quite generally also among the unchurched. It was this, more than anything else, which led the frontier Baptists to repudiate completely a salaried ministry, as the Quakers had done before them. They held that the ineffectiveness of the Anglican clergy of the southern colonies, particularly, was due to their paganized and corrupt dogmas, which they used to exploit the people, and to the fact that they were in the ministry for what they could get out of it. The continual denunciations of the corruptions of Christianity in the writings of the intellectual liberals in the interest of a pure and simple Christianity which the common man could understand and accept played no little part in popularizing the Jeffersonian crusade.

The eighteenth century has been called the skeptical era in modern history. Its character was produced by causes more practical than speculative, "more moral than intellectual, less theological than ecclesiastic." All over western Europe as well as in America there were religious insurrections whose causes were more political and social than metaphysical. The revolt was less from Christianity than from the church; or, perhaps it may be stated, it was a revolt from Christianity because of the church. The intellectual liberals had their part to play in it, but without the support of the common people its great achievement, the separation of church and state and complete religious liberty, would have been impossible.

One of the greatest contributions, if not the greatest one, which America has made in the realm of politics as well as in religion, has been the complete separation of church and state and the achievement of religious liberty. It is assumed by most Americans that the question of the relation of religion to the state has been solved, as far as we are concerned, once and for all; that the destruction of religious freedom which has been taking place in other parts of the world need not concern us. But the great freedoms cannot be taken for granted, even in this land of the free. If this basic freedom of all of our freedoms, freedom of conscience, is being challenged anywhere, it is in danger everywhere. We need to be fully aware of the fact that there are powerful reactionary forces at work in the world today that would do away with it. A pastoral letter of the archbishops and bishops of Peru, read in all the Catholic churches in that republic, completely repudiates the principle of religious freedom and asserts the outworn medieval theory that religious solidarity is essential to the stability of civil government. And there can be no doubt that this un-American conception has widespread acceptance even here in our own land. This fact should make us eternally vigilant and should cause us to bear in mind that no great and good cause is ever finally and completely won.

4

METHODIST UNIFICATION

THE most disastrous divisions that have ever occurred in American Protestantism have been those which have come about as the result of the great slavery controversy. From about the year 1830 to the close of the Civil War the slavery issue dominated the political, economic, social, and religious thinking of the nation. These were also years of rapid expansion of the American churches. And those churches which succeeded in developing the most adequate methods of following population as it pushed westward became the most widely planted and evenly distributed religious bodies in the nation. Thus the Presbyterians, the Baptists, and the Methodists, the three most successful churches in American Protestantism from the standpoint of gaining members, were to be found more or less evenly distributed throughout the country, east and west, north and south. It was their even distribution throughout the entire nation which rendered these religious bodies particularly susceptible to sectional controversy. So it came about that when the slavery issue divided the nation into an antislavery North and proslavery South, these evenly distributed churches likewise split into proslavery and antislavery divisions. Sectional churches, such as the Congregational, were able to avoid a slavery schism because they had been from the beginning confined to one section, the North.

Of the three evenly distributed churches the Presbyterians were the first to experience a major division. In 1837-38 they divided into Old School and New School bodies. Slavery, however, was only one of several issues responsible for this first major schism in American Protestantism. In general, the causes of that division arose out of the stream of Congregational influence which flowed into Presbyterianism as a result of the Plan of Union of 1801, whereby the Presbyterians and the Congregationalists agreed to work together on the frontier. Nor was the Old School-New School division a clear-cut sectional split; but there is no doubt, in the light of recent studies of the issues involved, that slavery played an important role in the final result. By the opening of the Civil War the Presbyterians had suffered two additional divisions when both Old School and New School churches divided into southern and northern bodies. Thus where there had been one Presbyterian church in 1836 there had come to be four in 1861. Unlike the Presbyterians, both the Baptists and the Methodists divided clearly over the slavery issue; and by 1845 this cleavage had resulted in the creation of distinct northern and southern bodies in both churches.

II

The healing of the sectional differences in all the churches might have been furthered immediately following the Civil War had it not been for the unfortunate reconstruction policies adopted by the federal government and the quite general concurrence in those policies by all the northern churches. At the close of the war the northern churches for the most part looked upon the South as a mission field; and instead of attempting to bring about some degree of co-operation with the southern brethren in meeting the peculiar problems of the postwar South, they began an aggressive policy of southern expansion. They were particularly active in carrying on work among the freedmen, more often than not in such a manner as to arouse southern resentment.

The southern activity of the northern churches, however, was not confined entirely to the Negroes. This was particularly true of the Methodists, who began at once to form conferences in those regions in the South where a strong Union sentiment had persisted. This invasion of the South by northern Methodists was somewhat matched by the southern Methodist invasion of the North, particularly on the Pacific coast. And in the long run, perhaps the presence of southern Methodists in the North and northern Methodists in the South was to prove one of the factors in the creation of better understanding, particularly after the passing of the reconstruction years.

At the close of the Civil War there was considerable talk, particularly on the part of certain northern leaders, of reunion of the churches North and South. This was at first generally resented in the South. The southern Methodist bishops in a pastoral letter issued in August,

1865, pointed out that "the talk of reunion of the two churches" is but a systematic attempt "already inaugurated . . . to disturb and if possible disintegrate and then absorb our membership individually. . . . Their [Methodist Episcopal] policy is eventually our division and ecclesiastical devastation." This opinion was concurred in by all the southern annual conferences as well as by all the southern church papers. That the letter represented correctly the position of certain northern Methodists is doubtless true, but the best leadership of the North was soon to manifest a very different attitude toward the southern brethren.

The first step toward a better understanding was taken by the bishops of the Methodist Episcopal Church at their episcopal meeting in 1869, when they sent three of their number to bear fraternal greetings to the southern bishops. This was the first exchange of such greetings since the separation in 1845, and led to the inauguration of the custom of exchanging fraternal delegates at the general conferences of the two Methodist bodies. The first exchange was made at the general conferences of 1872 and 1874 respectively. This led to the creation by both bodies of commissions which met at Cape May, New Jersey, in 1876. There a basis of fraternity was unanimously adopted.

It is a significant fact that in all the early endeavors toward better understanding between the two Methodisms the bishops in every case took the lead, and that they continued to do so throughout the following years. This leadership may be epitomized in the persons of Bishop Eugene R. Hendrix of the Methodist Episcopal Church, South and Bishop Earl Cranston of the Methodist Episcopal Church. Both men came to look upon the furthering of the unification of American Methodism as the most important interest of their lives and the most significant phase of their work, and both died with the hope and expectation of its speedy accomplishment. Undoubtedly one of the reasons why unification has lagged among Baptists and Presbyterians is that they both have lacked the type of leadership the Methodists have had in their bishops.

III

As a whole southerners have been more conservative than their northern brethren. This is a part of their heritage carried over from the prewar period when the whole South was on the defensive. The necessity of upholding their peculiar institution, slavery, rendered them abnormally sensitive to criticism of any sort, especially from outsiders, and led naturally to the suspicion that all new ideas were dangerous. As a result freedom of thought and expression was largely suppressed, and there are even yet certain taboos in the South which everyone recognizes. Dr. Eaton, in his recent study, *Freedom of Thought in the Old South,* has pointed out that none of the "isms" so common in the North, whether political, social, economic, or religious, has ever found a foothold in the South. This taboo of everything new in the South has been one of the barriers which have kept the northern and southern churches apart. The Social Gospel is a case in point. This emphasis found a much larger acceptance in the North than in the South, while on the other hand the old type of revivalism has persisted to a much larger degree in the South than in the North. It would seem, however, from numerous indications that southern Methodists have rid themselves more largely than any other southern religious body of the old sectional attitudes.

One factor which has appreciably aided southern Methodists in getting away from the old sectionalism has been the new educational influence. The founding of four new Methodist universities in the South within the last two generations has been a powerful liberalizing influence. Vanderbilt University, opened in 1875, was in a sense the first real southern university, and its school of religion was the first theological institution of southern Methodism. Although the official relationship of Vanderbilt with the church was severed in 1914, nevertheless during the forty years in which it was the principal Methodist university in the South it turned out an increasingly influential leadership for the church, and its clientele is still strongly Methodist.

The opening of Southern Methodist University at Dallas, Texas, and the transforming of Emory College into Emory University and Trinity College into Duke University, each of them with its school of religion, have given southern Methodism the undoubted leadership in southern theological education. All of these universities have a national outlook, while their faculties and students have been increasingly drawn from all sections of

[69]

the country. To a large extent southern Methodist leadership in unification came either directly or indirectly out of these new university centers. And in formal educational equipment, the southern Methodist leaders had in many respects the edge on their northern brethren who occupied similar positions in their respective churches at the time of unification.

Another interesting fact that helps explain the changing situation in southern Methodism is that for the last generation southern Methodist students have gone increasingly to the Yale Divinity School or to the divinity school of the University of Chicago, and not a few of the present-day leaders in southern Methodism have advanced degrees from these two institutions.

Such have been some of the influences which have been at work within southern Methodism breaking down the old sectional prejudices and undermining the old taboos.

IV

American Methodists, whether North or South or Methodist Protestant, have never lost sight of their common historical heritage. John and Charles Wesley, Francis Asbury, William McKendree, and a host of other early Methodist worthies were held in equal reverence by all branches of American Methodists throughout all the vicissitudes of controversy and division. When both branches of Episcopal Methodists formed young people's societies in the nineties, both adopted the name "Epworth League" in commemoration of the birthplace of John Wesley. When the Methodist Episcopal church chose "Abingdon Press" as the trade name of its Book Concern in commemoration of the seat of the first American Methodist college, the southern Methodists selected "Cokesbury Press" as the trade name of their publishing house in commemoration of the college founded at Abingdon. And so it has been throughout the years, each branch rivaling the other in doing honor to the great Methodist names and events of the past. Thus both of the major divisions of American Methodists have continued increasingly conscious of their common historic standing ground.

This fact is clearly stated in the pastoral address before the second Ecumenical Conference held in Washington in 1891, at which the Methodist Protestants as well as the two branches of Episcopal Methodism were represented. On the question of Methodist union the address states:

We rejoice to recognize the substantial unity which exists among the various Methodist Churches. Its firm basis is a common creed. We are all faithful to the simple, scriptural, and generous theology which God, through the clear intellect and loving heart of John Wesley, restored to his Church. . . . And there are other grounds of unity. We are proud of the same spiritual ancestry; we sing the same holy hymns; our modes of worship are similar; and what is most important of all, the type of religious experience is fundamentally the same throughout the Methodist world. Our ecclesiastical principles are not so various as the forms in which they are accidentally embodied. Rejoicing in these things, we think that the time has come for a closer cooperation of the Methodist Churches, both at home and abroad, which shall prevent waste of power and unhallowed rivalry; while before the eyes of many of us has passed the delightful vision of a time when, in each land where it is planted, Methodism shall become, for every useful purpose, one, and the Methodism of the world shall be a close and powerful federation of churches for the spread of the kingdom of Christ.

This knowledge of a common past has undoubtedly played its part in keeping alive a spirit of unity among the various Methodist bodies in America.

There have been those, however, who have maintained that one way to promote Methodist unity is to forget the past, especially the controversial phases of Methodist history. In the year 1912 a manuscript dealing with the Methodist church and the Civil War was submitted to the Methodist Book Concern in New York for publication. The book editor, later to become one of the bishops of the Methodist Episcopal church, finally returned the manuscript to the author with the statement that since a plan of unification was under consideration by the two great branches of American Methodism, he thought it unwise to bring up the old issues that had caused division.

The book editor evidently proceeded on the assumption that unification could be furthered by forgetting all the old issues out of which controversy and division had come. But this assumption is fallacious in general, and was particularly so in the case of American Methodism. The chief drawback to the assumption is the fact that the defeated side does not forget. The first plan of unification which came to a vote in both branches of episcopal Methodism was defeated very largely because certain southern leaders had *not* forgotten the old issues, and especially the treatment which the southern church had received at the hands of its northern brethren following the war. All this came as a surprise to the northern Methodists. They had forgotten it. For it is easy for the victorious side to forget. But all the unpleasant facts which attended the reconstruction years, particularly, were vivid memories in the South. The taking over of southern Methodist church property and the lawsuits to regain it were recalled; and a campaign to defeat unification, based largely on the old issues, was carried on by certain southern leaders. It would seem, therefore, that the only way to deal with the past is neither to attempt to forget it, nor to ignore it, but rather to come to an understanding about it.

One of the principal influences which made Methodist unification possible was the growing historical-mindedness among the leaders of the three Methodist bodies which came together in 1939 to form the new Methodist church. By historical-mindedness I mean the willingness to consider all sides of all the historic issues which had caused division. Within the last fifty years both northern and southern Methodists, as well as the Methodist Protestants, have come more and more to accept the same historical viewpoints in regard to the former controversies and differences. Here is a noble example of the practical value of history, for the creation of historical-mindedness among American Methodists has been the accomplishment of the trained historian dealing with these controversial issues.

Fifty years ago there was not a single account of the slavery controversy in the church which had not been written to defend one side or the other. And the same thing was true of the issues out of which came the Methodist Protestant body. In fact, up until recent years American church history as a serious scholarly enterprise was simply nonexistent. There were, it is true, denominational histories in abundance, but all of them with few if any exceptions had been written by denominational leaders and for the purpose of denominational propaganda. They could all have been lumped under the head of patriotic history, prepared for the purpose of making the several denominational bodies think well of themselves. A good share of them were frankly and openly controversial, written to perpetuate differences and justify division rather than to heal the old wounds. It was the entrance of the trained historian into the field of American church history which gradually transformed the whole approach.

About the year 1912 the first doctor's dissertations in the field of American church history began to appear in the major American universities. But it was a good many years after that date before American church history subjects were accepted as a matter of course as doctoral dissertations in the graduate schools, the assumption being that it was impossible to deal with such subjects with a sufficient degree of objectivity. Dr. J. Franklin Jameson in his presidential address before the American Historical Association nearly forty years ago pointed out that American church history was a virgin field for the historical student. Since that time American church history has become universally recognized as a legitimate interest among historical scholars, and a long list of doctoral dissertations in that field have appeared at all the major American universities.

Two dissertations which have had a particular bearing upon Methodist division are *The Schism in the Methodist Episcopal Church, 1844,* by Professor John H. Norwood, published in 1923, and *Episcopal Methodism and Slavery* by Charles B. Swaney, published in 1926. The former was a dissertation prepared at Cornell University. The author was a non-Methodist and not even American born. But the study was so understanding, the judgments were so fair, and the author's appreciation of the problems the church faced was so sincere, that it was at once accepted by historians as a model of impartiality. The latter dissertation was prepared at Northwestern University and was a study of the whole impact of Negro slavery on Episcopal Methodism. Besides these two dissertations bearing directly on the slavery controversy in Methodism there have been several others dealing with other phases of Methodist history. Two that might be mentioned are Posey's *Beginnings of Methodism in the Old Southwest,* prepared at Vanderbilt University, and R. W. Goodloe's *The Office of Bishop in Episcopal Methodism,* prepared at the University of Chicago. Such studies as these performed the spadework for the rewriting of American Methodist history.

In 1933 the present writer published his *Methodism in American History.* It had been prepared at the request of the Commission on Courses of Study of the

Methodist Episcopal Church as one of the required books for ministerial training. In that volume all the controversial issues were treated objectively and in the light of such research as that furnished by special studies like those mentioned above. The author had no side to defend, no party to uphold. His object was to tell the whole truth without fear or favor and with full appreciation of all the differing viewpoints. Within a short time after the appearance of the book it not only was listed in the course of study for ministerial training in the Methodist Episcopal Church, but also was adopted by the Methodist Episcopal Church, South, as a required book in its list for ministerial preparation; and it found full acceptance by the Methodist Protestants. The three Methodist churches which united in 1939 had come to the place where they were able to accept a common viewpoint on all the old controversial issues over which they had divided.

The significance of this fact in its bearing on the achievement of unification of American Methodism is difficult to overestimate. It meant that the three Methodist bodies were no longer divided over the old issues. It did not mean necessarily that they had come to a full agreement regarding them all, but that such disagreements as remained were no longer divisive factors. It meant that each of them had come to a full appreciation of the others' viewpoints; in other words, unification was made possible not because the old issues had been forgotten, but rather because they were now fully understood.

It is difficult to see how unification can come about among Baptists and Presbyterians on any other basis. For they have the same differences in viewpoint on past issues to compose as had the Methodists. One of the reasons why unification lags in both bodies is that they lack historical-mindedness. And this lack exists largely because neither church has had the benefit of full-length historical studies, made by trained historians, of the issues out of which came the divisions. There have been several excellent studies of phases of the Presbyterian controversy, such as Hightower's *Joshua L. Wilson: Frontier Controversialist*, Moore's *R. J. Breckenridge*, and Vander Velde's *The Presbyterian Church and the Federal Union*, but they are all very recent and only Vander Velde's study is in print. The Baptists have still farther to go to achieve any degree of full understanding of their past issues.

Agitation for church union based upon present exigencies only is futile; for those who advocate this basis for union have proceeded too often on the assumption that the past is to be forgotten. Because they know little or nothing about the old controversial issues which have divided Christendom, they assume that everyone is equally ignorant. For that reason what they write and speak on church union is superficial. They fail to understand that church union can be achieved only on the basis of a full understanding of all the issues that have caused division.

5

THE CHURCH, THE SECT, AND THE CULT IN AMERICA

THE terms *church*, *sect*, and *cult* are frequently used as if they were synonymous and interchangeable. This loose usage tends to confuse three different types of religious organization and expression. The terms *sect* and *cult* are often applied disparagingly to certain religious bodies and religious movements. In the minds of many people the term *sect* implies an ignorant, over-emotionalized, and fanatical group; an ephemeral, fly-by-night movement that is here today and gone tomorrow. The term *cult* is considered even less respectable and implies a religious aberration, a faddist movement, or the followers of some new, self-appointed prophet or healer who promises new insight into long-hidden truth. The term *church*, on the other hand, implies a dignified, well-ordered body whose roots reach far into the past.[1]

[1] There have been a number of attempts to classify religious groups on the basis of social characteristics. Among them is Ernst Troeltsch's *Social Teaching of the Christian Church* (English translation by Olive Oyon, London, 1931). Troeltsch makes the fundamental distinction between church and sect hinge on the question of attitude toward society. The church is all-inclusive; men are born into it, they do not become members by voluntary choice; it accepts the secular order and becomes an integral part of the existing social structure. The sect, on the other hand, is a voluntary group made up of members who join by voluntary choice. Leopold von Wiese and Howard Becker, in *Systematic Sociology* (New York, 1932), pp. 624-42, classify religious

Neither the *sect* nor the *cult* is a new phenomenon. Both are as old as organized religion, and both appeared in the first century of Christianity. Each had a long history before it made its appearance within American Protestantism.

Generally speaking, out of the right-wing phase of Protestantism which emerged from the Reformation came the Protestant churches; out of the left-wing came the sects. Or to put it another way—there have always been three distinct emphases in Christianity; first, Christianity as an organization; second, Christianity as a creed or a body of belief; third, Christianity as a way of life. The right-wing type of Protestantism stressed Christianity as an organization and as a body of belief, whereas the left-wing type gave chief attention to Christianity as a way of life and considered organization and creed to be secondary. This does not mean that right-wing Protestantism gave no attention to Christian-

---

bodies into four types: (1) the *ecclesia* or church type, (2) denominations, (3) sects, and (4) cults, and defines each in terms of social function and in relation to general culture. An essential for an *ecclesia* or church is its close tie to the state. Since there is no state church in the United States there is no *ecclesia* or church here. Denominations are sects in an advanced state of social development. A sect is an exclusive minority group which has not made peace with the world. A cult is a loosely organized group whose primary interest is in securing a personal ecstatic experience which brings with it peace of mind and physical and mental health.

(The above statement is largely based on a paper by Professor Rupert Vance on "Church Types and Social Structure" presented before a conference on Religion in American Life under the auspices of the American Council of Learned Societies, Chicago, April 23-24, 1950.)

[79]

ity as a way of life, but rather that its accent was upon organization and creed, while Christianity as a way of life was more or less taken for granted.

II

The right-wing types of Protestantism, out of which came the Protestant churches, were all conservative movements, which did not entirely repudiate the past, but rather found in it a firm standing ground. They preserved many of the practices, beliefs, and modes of worship of the ancient and medieval church, discarding only the elaborate penitential system which had been built up by the medieval church, and which had been the principal cause of the corruptions that had engulfed Roman Catholicism. Lutheranism, Calvinism, Zwinglianism, and Anglicanism were all conservative, middle-class movements.

Out of these "classical" or right-wing Protestant movements came the Protestant state churches: the Lutheran state churches in the northern German states and in the Scandinavian countries; the Calvinistic-Zwinglian state churches in southern Germany, in the Protestant cantons of Switzerland, and in Holland; and the Presbyterian church of Scotland. In England, Anglicanism emerged. The state-church pattern still dominates in western European Protestantism, a fact which makes it difficult for European Protestant leaders to understand American Protestantism. Here in the New World left-wing Protestantism is much more significant; in Europe it has a low rating and is largely ignored.

A characteristic of the church is its emphasis upon an official creed or confession of faith. Churches are *confessional* bodies. Thus the Lutherans have their unalterable Augsburg Confession; the Reformed church has its Heidelberg Confession; the Dutch church its Confession of the Synod of Dort; the Presbyterians have their Westminster Confession; and the Church of England has its Thirty-nine Articles. Though in every case these several confessions were supposedly drawn from the Scriptures, yet to the left-wing Protestants they were all man-made.

The practice of infant baptism is also a church characteristic. All the so-called classical bodies were infant baptizers, and infant baptism came to signify initiation not only into the church but also into citizenship. This meant that church membership became a matter of course for all, or to put it another way, the churches tended to be all-inclusive in their membership, rather than selective or exclusive. Thus churches are large, and their discipline is apt to be loose or almost nonexistent, except perhaps in dealing with heresy.

Elaborate church polity is another church characteristic. All the right-wing Protestant bodies adopted either synodical or episcopal types of church government. Thus the church type tended to lay emphasis upon organization and ecclesiastical machinery; and the high officials were not concerned with spiritual matters alone, but were state officials classed, in England, as Lords. Under these conditions the religious life of a people dominated by an official church tended to become formal and impersonal, and religion was expressed in outward form. Thus religion tended to become externalized and institutionalized.

III

The sect emphasis has had a legitimate place in historic Christianity, and especially in the Protestant tradition. The characteristics of the sect, generally speaking, are just the opposite of those of the church. What the church affirms, the sect denies.

Classical Protestantism accepted and practiced the state church principle, whereas the sects, with complete unanimity, rejected both the principle and the practice of state churchism. The sects based their objection to state churches on the example of the early church, as set forth in the New Testament, and also on the ground that religion is a personal matter between the individual and God and that therefore no authority under heaven has the right to interfere with that relationship. It is a significant fact that such seventeenth- and eighteenth-century thinkers as John Locke and Thomas Jefferson accepted this principle as a truism, and as one of the rights that belong to men under the law of nature. Consequently, the principle was written into our Declaration of Independence and into the fundamental law of the land.

A second sect characteristic is opposition to all creeds and confessions of faith. The sect holds that the Bible is the only rule of faith and practice. In a sense this is a fundamental Protestant principle, since every article in every creed or confession of faith is based upon Scripture; but the sect repudiates these man-made digests. As a consequence most sects, having no all-inclusive statement of Bible teaching, as have the churches, tend to stress some one particular doctrine such as holiness or millenialism. This has been true of all Protestant sects from the beginning, and is illustrated today by such groups as the Church of God, the Assemblies of God, the Pilgrim Holiness, and the Seventh-Day Adventists.

A third sect characteristic is rejection of infant baptism. In every instance the sect holds to what is termed believer's baptism, or baptism after a person reaches the age of accountability. With few exceptions the sect considers immersion as the only true, scriptural mode of baptism.

Still another characteristic of sects is the exclusive nature of their membership. Admission to membership is based on the confession of a personal religious or conversion experience. This requirement in itself provides an effective screening of members. It was this factor in early colonial Congregationalism which kept the church membership small and extraordinarily exclusive. These were "gathered" churches, made up of people who had been gathered out of the "world."

Naturally, since the sect lays principal stress upon religion as a way of life, rather than upon religion as an organization and a creed or body of belief, it is strict in discipline. Instead of being inclusive in their membership, as are the churches, the sects are exclusive and therefore tend to be small. Church membership in countries where there were state churches tended to become the usual and matter-of-course thing; sect membership demanded a significant personal decision. Church membership is relatively easy to obtain; sect membership is achieved as a result of an inner emotional experience. You join a church with but little difficulty, and once in, you remain in for life, often without doing much about it. It is difficult to acquire sect membership, and to retain it one must manifest his fitness by his everyday life.

Since the sect places little stress upon organization, it tends toward simple forms of polity. Pretty generally the sects are congregational and with no overhead control. Some of them do not even keep membership rolls —they are kept in heaven. It is significant that almost half of the nearly three hundred religious bodies in the United States have the congregational type of polity, an indication of the widespread sect influence in this regard. And finally the sect tends to be short lived, often merging with other like groups. If it survives over a relatively long period of time, it tends to develop church characteristics.[2]

[2]Braden adds these further characteristics of sects which are in line with those given above: Sects are likely to be local rather than national in scope; they usually have no well-rounded institutions, educational or otherwise; they stand aloof from all interdenominational co-operative enterprises. Charles S. Braden, "The Sects," in "Organized Religion in the United States," *Annals of the American Academy of Political and Social Science*, CCLVI (March, 1948), 53-62.

Since the sects place little emphasis upon organization, they have little interest in bringing about a union of Protestantism. There is no sect concern, nor will there be, in the ecumenical movement, now receiving so much attention among the Protestant churches.

Because the sect type of religious organization is simple and easy to form, it appeals to simple people who have little or no historic sense. And since sects arise out of immediate human needs they tend to multiply in times of social and economic stress.

IV

Sect movements which have arisen in churches constitute one of the significant phases in the development of Protestantism in particular, but are not confined to Protestantism only. Sect movements of great importance have arisen in Catholicism, as well as in non-Christian religions. Monasticism, which may be defined as a system of living apart from the world, has numerous sect characteristics. Every monastery was, in a sense, a "gathered congregation," gathered out of the world. The monk was the "good man" of the Middle Ages, with his emphasis upon religion as a way of life, not as a creed or an organization.

Another example of a sect movement in Roman Catholicism is Jansenism, a movement which arose in seventeenth-century France. Starting as a protest against scholastic theology, which it denounced as anything but evangelical, it held that religion was something to be experienced, that such experience came through conversion, and that experience was much more important than reason as a guide. The Jansenists set out to revitalize the Church of Rome, not to overthrow it; but their movement, like many similar movements in Protestantism, was officially condemned. Nevertheless, it managed to maintain a toe hold in the church in out-of-the-way rural parishes and a few obscure monasteries.

The two greatest sect movements which have arisen in Protestantism are Pietism and Methodism. Pietism began as a movement within German Lutheranism in the latter part of the seventeenth century, and like almost all such movements arose as a protest against deadness and formalism in the German state churches. Its beginning date may be placed at 1670, when Philip Jacob Spener, the Lutheran pastor at Frankfort-on-the-Main, formed from among the more earnest of his congregation a little group which met twice a week at his home, there to read and discuss the Bible and to engage in prayer and the singing of hymns.

Thus arose the *Collegia Pietatis,* or the societies of piety. The movement spread to other parishes, and thence to every section of Germany. It was taken over by the German Reformed people, swept into the Scandinavian countries, and was brought to England, where it exercised a strong influence on Methodism. It became the dominant influence in Moravianism through Count Zinzendorf, a pietistic Lutheran, who became a Moravian bishop; was brought to the American colonies by German immigrants; and played a large part in starting the colonial revivals. It was a living source from which proceeded works of Christian charity, missionary enterprises, the care of orphans, the spreading of the Bible among the masses of the common people, and the instruction of the neglected.

There came to be two great pietistic centers in Germany, the University of Halle and Herrnhut in Saxony, the former the fountainhead of Lutheran Pietism, the latter the home of Moravian activity. Pietism started a new emphasis upon the Bible in theological education, and inspired a great burst of interest in hymn-writing and singing. Many of the best hymns in all our evangelical hymnals come from this period. Zinzendorf himself wrote more than a thousand hymns, and exercised a strong influence on the hymn-writing of the Wesleys. Since Pietism emphasized a religion of the heart, it naturally gave rise to religious poetry and song. Moravian worship, for instance, came to consist largely of antiphonal singing, and the Moravians made a greater contribution to sacred music than any other religious group in the American colonies.

Fortunately Pietism created few, if any, schisms in the Old World; but when transplanted to America it contributed to the formation of the two German churches which have only recently consummated a union, the United Brethren in Christ and the Evangelical church.

Methodism began as a sect movement within the Church of England, and John Wesley to the day of his death refused to consider it as anything else but a movement to revive "scriptural holiness" within the Anglican body. The idea of a possible separation from that church was abhorrent to him, and even more so to his brother Charles.

Methodism and Pietism had many things in common. Both grew out of a desire to revive religion in the state church; both stressed religion as an inner personal experience; both carried on their work by forming small groups of earnest people, drawn out of the churches; both were led by men of education who were opposed to fanatical and overemotionalized manifestations. Pietism had its main influence among the Lutheran and Reformed churches on the Continent; Methodism was confined to the British Isles in its beginning. Both, however, were brought to America by eighteenth-century immigrants, and both had a share in feeding the Colonial Awakenings—Pietism at the beginning, Methodism at the end.

Unfortunately churches have generally been antagonistic to sect movements within them. It is true that toward the end of John Wesley's life he had won the support of numerous Anglican clergymen, and had more invitations to preach in Anglican pulpits than he could accept; yet he never won the support or even the encouragement of the hierarchy. It was because the Bishop of London had refused to ordain even one of his preachers for America, where the Anglican clergy had refused to co-operate with his preachers in administering the sacraments to the Methodist people, that Wesley was forced to assume the right to ordain, and thus brought about a schism.

V

There is no better example of the process by which a sect develops into a church than that furnished by the Methodists. Although at the beginning Methodism was undoubtedly a sect movement, it has few sect characteristics today. This is particularly true of American Methodism. When Methodism became an independent ecclesiastical body in America at the close of the Revolution, it adopted Articles of Religion, which were simply the Thirty-nine Articles of the Church of England boiled down to twenty-five. Thus from the beginning it possessed a formal statement of belief.

In the second place, although John Wesley always insisted that Methodism was following the primitive church, yet he also insisted that his followers remain in the Anglican communion and receive the sacraments there. When the American Methodists separated from the Church of England, Wesley himself prepared a liturgy for them in which is preserved much that came out of the medieval church. The Methodist hymnal also is the product of the Christian centuries, as is Methodist ritual. Methodism has always practiced infant baptism, although immersion is optional, as it is in the Church of England. Although Methodism adopted the doctrine of conversion, it has never insisted upon it as a condition of membership. And certainly no one will ever accuse Methodism of having a simple form of church government. Lastly, Methodism in point of size does not qualify as a sect. Methodism formerly stressed the poor men's doctrines, holiness and conversion, but no longer are these doctrines preached in the best Methodist pulpits, although officially lip service is given to them.

Several American religious bodies are now in the transitional stage from sect to church. The Church of the Nazarene furnishes an example. Largely stemming from Methodism, it was formed in 1894 in Southern California by the union of several holiness bodies which had come out of the same general background of discontent with the trend of Methodism away from the holiness and sanctification emphasis. Organized on the Methodist model, it has all the Methodist characteristic machinery, only slightly modified. Since 1906 its growth has been rapid and it has spread over the United States, with congregations now in every state of the Union. The early Nazarene colleges, such as the "Nazarene Holiness College," all had in their names the term "Holiness"; today none of these colleges are so designated. The Nazarenes now stress an educated ministry, have recently opened a theological seminary in Kansas City, and are sending their brightest young men to the graduate schools to prepare them for professorships. Their service is also becoming more formal. The Pilgrim Holiness is another sect that is rapidly tending toward such a transformation, but it has not as yet gone as far as have the Nazarenes.

Economic cleavages are undoubtedly a large factor in the formation of sects. Churches tend to become upper-classish, and it is an unfortunate fact that Protestant churches of whatever kind seem to be unable to minister to all levels of society. All the so-called classical or right-wing Protestant bodies began as middle-class and conservative movements, and quite generally they have remained so even down to our own time.

The sect's emphasis upon religion as a way of life has determined the nature of its contributions. Freedom of conscience and its corollaries, freedom of speech, freedom of the press, separation of church and state, and full religious liberty—in fact all our great freedoms—we in America owe to a considerable degree to the sect principle that religion or the duty which we owe to God is a private concern with which no overhead authority has a right to interfere. We owe little to the churches in the achievement of our great basic freedoms; we owe much to the sects. In their attitudes toward freedom of conscience and church-state relationship, all the American Protestant bodies, churches and sects alike, have now adopted the sect principle. Historically the sect has a clear record as far as persecution is concerned; the church has not.

Since the sects stress Christianity as a way of life, they naturally oppose everything which tends to degrade and besmirch life. Their members must walk the straight and narrow path. In most instances, they make up the forces back of such reform movements as the temperance crusade. On such matters the churches are likely to be lukewarm, especially those churches in which there have been no sect movements. The Quakers offer a good example of a sect which, as Rufus Jones says, never takes a passive attitude toward any human wrong. This accounts for their leadership in all good causes to uplift and purify human life.

One of the principal reasons why churches are often antagonistic to sects and sect movements within churches is that sects tend to become fanatical, overstressing one doctrine or type of doctrine while understressing others, and tend to withdraw within themselves. Too often they are very critical of others who do not agree with them, and as a result are difficult to live with, glory in their exclusiveness, and develop a holier-than-thou complex. The statement has been made that the sects contribute by draining off the troublemakers. If this is said seriously, it represents a superficial point of view, and indicates that the real historic contributions of the sects are not understood.

VI

A *cult* is a religious group which looks for its basic and peculiar authority outside the Christian tradition. Generally cults accept Christianity, but often only as a halfway station on the road to greater "truth," and profess to have a new and additional authority beyond Christianity. This new authority may be a new revelation which constitutes additional "scriptures," or it may be an inspired leader who announces that he or she has gained additional insight into "truth."[3]

The largest and most important of the American cults is Mormonism. It is listed as a cult because it is definitely based upon what the Mormons believe to be a new revelation—the Book of Mormon. Though the Bible occupies a central place in Mormonism, the Book of Mormon is considered of divine authenticity and of equal authority with the Jewish Scriptures. The Mormons have also two additional books of revelations, the *Doctrines and Covenants* and the *Pearl of Great Price*. Now numbering more than a million members in the United States, Mormonism ranks among the twenty largest religious bodies in the nation. For that reason alone, if for no other, it needs to be better understood by the average American.

Next in importance among American cults is Christian Science. It is classed as a cult because it considers *Science and Health* a new discovery of truth and an absolute necessity for a correct understanding of the Bible. But Mary Baker Eddy is spoken of not as a "revelator" but as a "discoverer" of new truth. All good Christian Scientists are devoted readers of the Bible, but it is always read in connection with the Key to the Scriptures—*Science and Health*. Mrs. Eddy stated that she had never intended to found a new religious body,

[3]Braden, *op. cit.*, makes no distinction between the *sect* and the *cult*, but gathers all religious bodies under the two heads "denominations" and "sects." This, it seems to me, oversimplifies a complex situation.

hoping that all the churches would accept her new discovery of divine truth; but she soon realized that it was necessary in order to propagate her divine science to establish a new church which she called Church of Christ Scientist.

Theosophy and New Thought represent a group of cults distinctive in that they combine influences from other world religions. Theosophy, the first of these cults to make its appearance in America, was introduced by a Russian noblewoman, Helena P. Blavatsky, in 1875. Professing to draw its doctrines from the scriptures of the "Trans-Himalayan Masters of Wisdom," it claimed to investigate the "hidden mysteries of Nature" and stimulate the psychic and spiritual powers latent in man. The World's Parliament of Religion held in connection with the Chicago World's Fair in 1893 brought several representatives from India, some of whom remained to form Yogoda societies where the Hindu system of philosophic meditation and asceticism, designed to effect the union of the devotee's soul with the universal spirit, was explained if not practiced.

Nowhere else in the United States have cults flourished as they have in Southern California. The sunny, even climate of the region has attracted an overplus of old and ailing people, and as a result the region has sprouted a welter of faith healing cults. Carey McWilliams states that when two people meet for the first time in Southern California the first question asked is "Where do you come from?" and the second question is "How do you feel?" Aimee Semple McPherson's

Four Square Gospel movement, a combination of perfervid evangelism, showmanship, and faith healing, which has its center in Los Angeles, is only one of a number of such movements which have taken root there and perhaps should be classed as half sect and half cult.

In 1900 Katharine Tingley, a native New Englander, established near San Diego, California, the Point Loma Theosophical Community. Through William Q. Judge, she had become acquainted with Theosophy while residing in New York. She came west to fulfil a dream she had long entertained of building "a white city in a land of gold beside a sunset sea." On a five-hundred-acre tract at Point Loma there was soon erected an astonishing collection of institutions, a School of Antiquity, a Theosophical University, a Greek Temple and Raja Yoga College, and the Iris Temple of Art, Music, and Drama. Here Mrs. Tingley reigned as a veritable oriental potentate. All this was made possible by money raised in the East and by sizable "love offerings" contributed by all persons who applied for entrance to the colony. At the heyday of the movement a membership of one hundred thousand was claimed, and the fame of Point Loma spread far and wide. Theosophists from everywhere began to converge upon the region. One of the early colonists at Point Loma was Albert Powell Warrington, a retired lawyer from Virginia, who soon had in what is now the middle of Hollywood a theosophical center rivaling Point

Loma, called Krotona, to which a remarkable collection of writers, mystics, and crackpots were attracted.[4]

For sheer audacity, even in the land of freak religious cults, the I AM cult is, to quote Carey McWilliams, the "weirdest mystical concoction" that has ever sprouted in the region. Its founders were Guy W. Ballard and his wife, Edna, the first an ex-paperhanger and the second an ex-medium. Ballard came to California in 1932, and in 1934 published, under a nom de plume, a treatise entitled *Unveiled Mysteries* in which the doctrines of the cult are set forth. The ascended Master of St. Germain is the deity of the cult, who mysteriously supplied Ballard with a cup of "pure electronic essence" and a wafer of "concentrated energy"; and on a trip around the world in the "stratosphere" with St. Germain as guide, Ballard located the places where the wealth of all the ages lies buried. The principal attraction of the Great I AM is the promise of wealth and power to the faithful. Through sales of *Unveiled Mysteries* at $2.50 a copy and of pictures of Ballard, phonograph records, I AM rings, and numerous other cult gadgets, some $3,000,000 had been collected at the time Mrs. Ballard was convicted of fraud by a federal court.

Another group of cults stemmed from the teachings of "Dr." P. P. Quimby, the friend and early teacher of Mrs. Eddy. Stressing health, happiness, and success,

[4]For a recent appraisal of the cult movements in Southern California, see Carey McWilliams, *Southern California Country* (New York, 1946), chap. xiii, "Don't Shoot Los Angeles," pp. 240-72.

these cults have attracted thousands of people throughout the country. Unity School of Christianity, with headquarters in Kansas City, is a thriving example of this type of appeal. Both Unity and "Psychiana," with headquarters in Moscow, Idaho, carry on their propaganda largely through excellently printed magazines and "lessons" which go out literally by the tens of thousands.

The Father Divine movement seems to belong in a class by itself. Begun among displaced Negroes in and around New York, it has spread into numerous northern cities, where it has attracted some whites as well as Negroes. Charles S. Braden characterizes the movement as "deeply religious" and a "remarkable social and economic movement which provides for its people a security and a sense of social worth and significance which they had never before known." But this should not disguise the fact that the movement is guilty of blatant blasphemy in holding that Father Divine is God.

The simplest explanation for the confusion of tongues which prevails in Southern California is to be found in the nature of the population. It is a land of migrants. Almost everyone seems to have but recently come from somewhere else. The people have broken old home ties; they have moved away from old friends, old community influences and restraints, as well as from the old church and the accustomed religious patterns. It is a well-established sociological fact that migrant peoples fail to carry cultural roots with them.

Like the children of Israel wandering in the wilderness, they erect for themselves "golden calves"; they build new altars in the desert of their wanderings. They have broken the old religious ties, and not finding in their new homes congenial relationships in their former churches or religious groups, are an easy prey to new and strange doctrines. And unfortunately the present-day migrants are rendered all the more vulnerable to the lure of strange gods by the fact that few have had any deep or adequate religious training.

A basic difference between the sect and the cult is that the sect carries on within the Christian tradition, the cult largely outside that framework. Cults like Mormonism and Christian Science have strong ties binding them to the Christian tradition. Ethical Culture accepts Christian ethics but rejects Christian theology. Mormonism and Christian Science call themselves churches and have many church characteristics. Perhaps another distinction between sects and cults is that the cult stresses health and happiness in this life; the sect stresses spiritual riches and heaven at last.

6

ECUMENICITY BEGINS AT HOME

Is ECUMENICITY more than just a word? Among ministers of all the great Protestant churches in America today it is undoubtedly a charmed word. In the first place it is a big word, and how ministers and theologians love to roll such terms under their tongues! But for that very reason the use of the term is, to a greater or lesser degree, self-defeating. In an effort to find out whether the word "ecumenicity" has any particular significance today among laymen, I made inquiry of several of my laymen friends. Although some of them knew the root meaning of the term, they were not sure just what it meant to ministers and theologians; and it is certain that the term had not carried with it a vision of world-wide Christianity and a universal Christian fellowship. At the ecumenical conference of Christian youth which met at Amsterdam just prior to the opening of World War I, the delegates were asked whether the ecumenical vision was preached and understood in their parish churches, and the reply was a resounding "No!"

I recall that during my theological seminary course, now a good many years in the past, the word *Zeitgeist* was almost indispensable in making a learned speech. It was one of the charmed words of that day. I have sometimes wondered why that term is so seldom used today, or whether its use ever resulted in anything other than the satisfaction it gave the user. But it was a wonderful word to tone up a speech. And I fear that the term "ecumenicity" is now being used in not a few instances for the same purpose; it, too, is a good word to tone up a speech.

There are many instances in the past of great and good causes that never succeeded in getting past the "word" and "resolution" stage. In the year 1816, for example, there was formed in the United States the American Colonization Society. Its purpose was to induce slave owners to free their slaves, provided they be sent to Africa. It was hoped that so many would respond that the society would become an effective force in causing slavery to disappear. From the start it had the support of the churches, and in their Synods, Associations, and Conferences resolutions were unanimously passed, year after year, endorsing the society. For several reasons the scheme soon proved to be a complete and even dismal failure. But the Synods, Conferences, and Associations kept right on passing resolutions endorsing it, even though it was universally known that the American Colonization Society was doing nothing at all to help solve the problem of Negro slavery in America. Undoubtedly the voting for such resolutions soothed many an uneasy clerical conscience, even though it did nothing else.

For most of us before the outbreak of World War I the peace movement was in the resolution stage; it was only a word. To many the race problem is in that stage now. Resolutions calling for the bettering of race relations receive unanimous support in all of our church assemblies—indeed, it would be a hardy individual who would dare to vote against them. But we know well enough that it is one thing to vote for such resolutions and quite another to do something about it. Far too many of us are praying "Thy kingdom come, but not now." Emotionally, we are all pro-ecumenical, but most of us are doing very little about it. It is something to be believed in; we make little real effort to translate belief into action. Not so long ago, I heard three Methodist bishops emphatically state that they would not tolerate in their respective areas any community or united church programs involving a Methodist church. Each of them, I am sure, would have repudiated hotly any hostility to the principle of church co-operation and union. They just did not want to be bothered with such experiments in their areas because it would involve and complicate Methodist administration. They accepted the idea of church co-operation but not the practice of it.

II

Ecumenicity must begin at home. There is no country in the world which calls more emphatically for the ecumenical emphasis than does the United States of America. With more than three hundred independent religious bodies we are divided "six ways for Sunday." Think of all the confessions of faith which have been evolved through the Christian centuries! They were intended to unite Christian people, but instead of uniting, they have served to set one group over against another. They have, in too many instances, simply served as fences to keep people apart, rather than as great uniting bonds. It is astonishing how such a matter as modes of baptism has caused controversy and division. The largest Protestant family in America is built around a rigid insistence upon a certain mode of baptism. Several of the divisions in Methodism, both in England and in America, have been precipitated by quarrels over church polity.

One might think that the acceptance of the Bible as the only rule of faith and practice, which is a basic sect characteristic, would be a strong unifying force. But not at all. There are more than a hundred bodies in the United States which accept this as their basic principle, but each has a separate string upon which it fiddles. Other bodies place chief stress on the apostolic succession, and have proceeded to set themselves rigidly apart from all others, claiming for themselves the only valid ministry. Thus the Roman Catholics set themselves apart and will not consider the possibility of cooperation with any other religious body, on the ground that they alone possess all Christian truth. A contemporary Roman Catholic authority says, "Any process of adjustment, conference, organization or any attempt at reconciliation, between the points of view of different churches is something entirely out of agreement with its conception of the Church itself." The Roman Catholic church is, it claims, in itself a perfect union; and any attempt to make adjustments to any other church, instead of creating a larger unity, would only destroy its own perfect unity. And so it goes on ad infinitum.

To a large degree we are divided over trivialities, as Harry Emerson Fosdick has pointed out. At least they are trivia when compared to the great basic principles of our Christian faith. The great universally accepted principles—that one must love God and love his neighbor as himself; that God has made of one blood all mankind; that love is the fulfilling of the law—these are ideals without boundaries. Neither race nor nation hems them in. Then why cannot we unite about these great Christian universals? It is a strange and sad fact that instead of centering our convictions and loyalties in these great universals of our common Christianity, we give our loyalty to petty and trifling matters. Did Jesus bring a conception of God too big for us? A Jewish scholar has stated that here we have the reason for which Jesus was rejected by the Jews. His conception of God was too big for his contemporaries. Is Jesus' conception of God too big for us, too?

One of our great sins in our contemporary situation is that we tend to mix the great Christian universals and our petty local peculiarities as though they were of equal importance. And too often the local loyalties hide the great universals. Today, as never before, we must determine to set ourselves to disentangle the Christian universals from the special settings and adhesions which have come from local cultures. Christianity faces a competition in the world today, upon the outcome of which depends the future of mankind. This is a time for greatness in religion and not for pettiness. And we may thank God for the Christian leadership which recognizes this fact as never before.

III

Protestantism in America has the chance now to set the ecumenical pace for the world.

In the first place, the United States is a religious microcosm; religiously we are an epitome of the world. Here are all the creeds of Christendom; here are all the types of church polity that have evolved throughout the Christian centuries. Lutheranism is here in all its varieties; twenty kinds are in the United States, all of them direct or indirect transplantations from the Old World. From Scotland and North Ireland have come the Presbyterians and with them have come their ancient differences and tensions. All the Eastern Orthodox churches to be found in Christendom are represented in the city of Chicago, together with the Uniat churches and practically all the linguistic divisions in Roman Catholicism. In 1947, on a certain Sunday in Chicago, the Roman Catholic mass was said in fourteen different rites. In other words, the United States has been, and still is, the draining sink for the world's religious differences and divisions.

We are accustomed to bemoan the great number of religious bodies in the United States, but the two basic reasons for this diversity are matters of pride. The first is that America has been from the beginning a haven of refuge for the distressed people of the world who have suffered for conscience; the second is that since independence we have had complete religious liberty. Old World divisions are, therefore, basically responsible for the religious diversity which we have in the United States, coupled with the fact that we have given all men equal rights under the law to worship as they please.

In almost every respect we are the most fortunately situated nation in Christendom for the achievement of the widest ecumenical ends. One reason why this is true is that there is no distinction in the eyes of the law between the American churches, of whatever name or kind. There are no privileged religious bodies; all have an equal right to exist and to carry on. Perhaps the greatest barrier to cordiality between the churches in Britain is the existence of the long tradition of an established church. And the same thing is true in every nation of Europe. The free churches just do not rate with the established bodies. Under such circumstances, there have naturally developed superiority and inferiority complexes creating cleavages which cannot be bridged by any amount of good intentions. I was informed by one who attended the Oslo Conference that the free churches of the continent of Europe had practically no part in that great gathering. One might suppose that the experience of the past half-generation would have changed attitudes; but, on the contrary, it seems that the old European patterns still persist.

The fact that the Episcopal and Congregational churches had been established churches in the colonial period hindered their normal development after independence. One of the reasons why they failed to grow in like proportion to the Baptists, the Methodists, and the Presbyterians, as the country expanded westward, was that they continued to maintain a superiority feeling which came as a consequence of their previous privileged position, and the strong feeling for equality on the frontier rendered them unpopular.

The disappearance of all legal inequalities among the American churches has been a basic factor in preparing the ground for closer church relationships. Nowhere else in the world does such a favorable situation prevail for the promotion of interchurch harmony and understanding as here in America. Complete equality of all religious bodies in the eyes of the law is one of our proudest traditions, and justly so.

The conception of the church which has come to prevail in American Protestantism is that of a voluntary society and not an authoritarian institution tied to the state. Its sacraments are means of grace rather than symbols of historic confessions. The great historic confessions of faith from the Council of Nicaea onward were often as much the result of political expediency as of the desire to promote the cause of religious truth. America has produced no great commanding declarations of faith, such as those which emerged out of post-Reformation controversies in Europe and which divided European Protestants into rigid doctrinal divisions and warring camps. There have been two instances in our history in which confessions of faith were drawn up partly as political symbols, and both came about as a result of the legal establishment of Congregationalism in New England. Complete disestablishment in America has saved us from making creeds and professions of faith political symbols, and thus a major factor in the creation of hard and fast religious distinctions was removed at the very beginning of our national existence.

IV

The long persisting influence of the American frontier exercised a great leveling power in every phase of American life—in religion as well as in society and politics. Equality was a catchword of great potency in the West, and has remained so to our own time. Although there were sharp differences in theology and church polity among the most successful frontier churches, yet their differences were often less in evidence than their likenesses. The religious diversity of the frontier was underlaid with a certain uniformity which made possible a large degree of unity of action. The frontier churches placed theology as distinctly secondary to the practical work which the needs of the frontier demanded, and they found it possible to work together in spite of their divergent views and polities. Their willingness to cooperate is shown by the rise, in the first third of the nineteenth century, of a large number of interdenominational agencies—the American Bible Society, the American Tract Society, the home missionary agencies, temperance societies, and many others. All the frontier evangelical churches were in full accord on the great moral issues, and they are in accord today.

The frontier religious bodies adopted also a common method of bringing Christianity to bear upon the moving and restless society pushing westward. That method was revivalism, and from the great colonial awakenings to Moody and Billy Sunday revivalism has been to a large degree interdenominational.

V

The cultural and educational gulf between the major Protestant churches has now all but disappeared. A hundred years ago, that gulf was deep and wide, and seemingly permanent and impassable. Less than a hundred years ago, in New England, Baptist and Methodist churches were described as thriving "upon the outcasts of society," while their preachers were noted for their "bad grammar, low idioms, and the euphony of a nasal twang in preaching." As far as Methodism is concerned, the social and cultural transformation has been too extreme, in that it has created other cleavages which make it increasingly difficult to reach the lower economic groups. This constitutes one of the most puzzling problems for our own time.

A century and more ago, there was a sharp distinction between the churches over the question of an educated ministry. It was naturally quite out of the question for an educated ministry to have much in common with an uneducated ministry. Today that distinction has largely faded, and ministers of all the major denominations now meet on the same cultural and educational plane. Theological education has become increasingly inter-denominational, and no church has broken over denominational lines in this regard to a greater degree than have the Methodists. According to figures compiled in 1947, there were then 676 Methodist students enrolled in non-Methodist theological seminaries and 48 Methodist instructors on the staffs of these institutions. Another interesting fact is that of these 676 Methodist students in non-Methodist seminaries, 326 were serving Methodist charges, an indication that a great majority of these students were in training for the Methodist ministry. The courses offered and the books used in all the seminaries of the Presbyterians, Congregationalists, Baptists, Methodists, Disciples, Evangelical and Reformed, and even of the Episcopalians and the United and Augustana Lutherans present an amazing degree of uniformity. Our English friends, attending the Methodist Ecumenical Conference in Springfield, found it difficult to understand this situation, and some of them were critical of it. Here, it seems to me, is an ecumenical influence of unusual importance. Although this indicates that the Methodists need to strengthen their seminaries, it also proves that Methodists are among the most ecumenical-minded.

Interdenominational religious journalism has played its part in creating a common point of view on many issues. This type of journalism began nearly a hundred years ago and has continued with an ever increasing influence. It is an interesting and revealing fact that Methodists constitute the largest single block of *Christian Century* subscribers.

Increasing historical-mindedness of the ministers of all the major Protestant bodies is one of the results of a better-trained ministry. The larger familiarity with historic Christianity has made us more conscious of the rich common heritage of the ages to which we are all heirs alike. In other words, we are finding in the past a common standing ground, and with it a new appreciation of the *church* and a lessening of the emphasis upon the *churches*.

Ecumenicity among the American churches has been a growing process which has been going on for more than a hundred years. We are apt to think of ecumenicity and church union in terms of recent interchurch conferences and formal resolutions, but seldom in terms of the underlying factors and forces which will make union possible when it is finally achieved. The vast destruction, both spiritual and moral, wrought by World War II has brought to American Protestantism a sense of duty and of mission such as it had never previously experienced. We face a world task which demands a united Protestantism, both here in America and throughout the world. The war and its aftermath have done much to bridge the chasm between the American and European churches, as well as between the major denominations in the American Protestant family. The times are ripe for a sweeping ecumenical achievement, and a needy world demands it.

INDEX

Abingdon Press, 71
Allen, Ethan, 53
American church history, development of, 74-77; doctoral dissertations in, 75-77
American churches, equal under the law, 106
Americanization, 2
Architecture, Dutch, 6
Aristotle, 31
Art, immigrant contributions to, 27

Baldwin, Alice M., quoted, 43
Baltimore, Lord, 40
Baptists, 62; and slavery, 64; Virginia, 61
Bible, only rule of faith and practice, 82, 102
Blavatsky, Helena P., 94
Braden, Charles S., quoted, 84, 93, 97

California, Southern, home of cults, 94-96; land of migrants, 97-98
Calvin, John, theories of government, 33, 35, 36
Chicago, University of, divinity school, 70
Christian Science, 93-94, 97
Christianity, three distinct emphases in, 79-80
Church: American Protestant conception of, 106; characteristics of, 81-82; Locke's definition of, 46; polity, types of, 81; and state, separation of, 50, 63

Church of England, 34
Civil War, 65-66
Cokesbury Press, 71
Confessions of faith, Protestant, 81
Cranston, Bishop Earl, 68
Crèvecoeur, Jean de, quoted, 3-4
Cult, the, characteristics of, 92-95
Cultural contributions of recent immigrants, 26-27
Cultural pluralism, definition of, 2

Danes, 22
Declaration of Independence, 82
Deism, two types of, 53, 54
Democracy: defined, 31; delayed in Roman Catholic lands, 36; and left-wing Protestantism, 36, 38; pioneering and, 38
Dewey, John, quoted, 41
Divine, Father, 97
Duke University, 69
Dunkers, 12, 14, 17
Dutch, influence of in America, 5-6
Dutch Reformed church, 5
Dutch West India Company, 5, 10

Early church, example of, 82
Eastern Orthodox churches, 25-26
Eaton, Clement, 68
Ecumenical Methodist Conference, 71-72
Ecumenical movement, the, 99-110

[111]